I0111302

All Scripture references taken from the KJV of the Holy Bible, unless otherwise indicated.

Get Out *of* Captivity

by Dr. Marlene Miles
Freshwater Press 2024
freshwaterpress9@gmail.com

ISBN: 978-1-965772-34-8

Paperback Version

Table of Contents

Get Out *of* Captivity

Freshwater Press, USA

Lord Jesus, You have come to heal the brokenhearted, to proclaim freedom for the captives and release from darkness for the prisoners, to proclaim the year of the LORD's favor and the day of vengeance of our God.

Introduction

Captivity is a big subject. Sometimes there is no quick, fast, and in a hurry way to say a thing or teach a thing. That is why there is a whole Bible to read and learn. That is why there is the Holy Spirit who is the Spirit of Wisdom and the Spirit of Knowledge and Understanding, and He will lead you into all Truth. That is why God gave *some teachers* and all of the five-fold ministry to impart knowledge to us. That is why we have parents who should have taught us *at all time*s, just as their parents should have done for them. That is why we live 100 or so years because we must try out this knowledge, Wisdom, discernment and understanding, to know what Captivity is and how to get delivered from it.

Sometimes deliverance is simply hearing the truth.

He hath sent me to preach deliverance to the captives. (Luke 4:18)

Deliverance can be obtained by hearing? By hearing preaching? That sounds good. Why don't more preachers preach deliverance, then?

If we get into Captivity, all this learning, information, teaching, discernment and empirical knowledge will help us get out. Hopefully, it won't take 100 years to escape, but we must get out before the end of our Earth years. To never get into captivity is the goal, but to get out and then help others out is noble, and it is God's work. You do not want to be the reason that your children or your *children's* children would be born, bred, have to live their lives, or be stuck in Captivity. Hey, a really good inheritance to leave your children is to make sure that you haven't put them in Captivity vis-à-vis your being stuck there.

This book will take us far, but not all the way because there is so much to know and there are so many ways that *captivity*, for example, can happen to a person or a people, or a nation.

And others save with fear, pulling *them* out of the fire; hating even the garment spotted by the flesh.
(Jude 1:23)

Deliver Us from Evil

Our Father which art in Heaven… deliver us from evil, for thine is the power and the glory forever, amen.(Matthew 6:9, 13)

Jesus taught His Disciples, and thereby us to pray. The Lord's prayer is a daily prayer. In it we pray for deliverance. Why might we need to pray for deliverance daily? Because daily we may sin, daily we may not repent, daily there are traps and snares set for us. Daily, and also nightly we may run the risk of being captured, ensnared, tricked, trapped, or taken captive.

Every morning there are tender mercies. *Why*? Because we might not even know what we did last night, in the dream, and in the spirit.

Some say that Christians do not need deliverance. If you are one of those people, read on anyway, even though this book is not to convince you, it is to inform my Dear Readers.

Lord, Give Us Deliverance

We want deliverance. We need deliverance--, well, those of us who can **see** ourselves. Those who hear the voice of the Holy Spirit--, yeah, we may be aware that we need deliverance. But those who are closed off and believe that there is absolutely nothing wrong with themselves will find it difficult to fathom that *they* need deliverance. No, it's *them*, it's *those* other people who need to change, be better, be different, or just go away. The nose blind will not seek deliverance. Instead, those are the people who seek *riddance*. In their hearts or even out loud they may say, "If we can just get rid of *those other people*--, they are the problem, they are my problem."

When you can't see that your problem is **you**, probably at least 99.9% of the time, then you are nose blind.

We need deliverance from what?

Captivity.

From where?

Captivity.

From whom?

Captivity.

How did we get into this situation?

Captivity.

When did these problems all start?

Captivity.

Captivity is a what, it is a where, it is a who, it is a how, and it also is a when. It spans the dimensions so we will talk about captivity quite a bit in this book, and we will talk about it in regard to time, and also in regard to dimensional captivity.

Most often I know most of what I will say and write in a book. Not this one. The Holy Spirit will be teaching me as I write. That means the Holy Spirit will also be teaching you. Thank God for the Holy Spirit. Thank God for ears to hear. Thank God for understanding. Amen.

Captivity is the problem; it might be the only problem. Everything that is wrong from birth to the grave is caused by Captivity. Adam and Eve sinned; they were kicked out of the Garden of Eden; they were kicked out into the land of curses where stuff just didn't work right anymore. God told them if they ate of that certain Tree they would surely die. They didn't die physically, but they died spiritually. Being dead spiritually, now they were able to be captured—they became candidates for Captivity.

Boldly, I say, anything outside of the Garden of Eden is spiritual jail. Anywhere outside of the Garden of Eden is Captivity. Outside the Garden was Captivity--, it was for Adam & Eve, and it was also for all of us-- until Jesus got here.

Captivity is a Person

Awake, awake, Deborah: awake, awake, utter a
song: arise, Barak, and led thy captivity captive,
(Judges 5:12A)

Wisdom is a person. She is referred to as *she*
many times in the Proverbs.

Time is a person. We refer to time as Father
Time; so Time will receive the pronoun, *he*.

Captivity is a person. *Jesus led Captivity
away.* Jesus didn't drag a prison or a concept, or a
building; Captivity is a Person.

Captivity is the warden of the spiritual prison
which is also named Captivity. The prison is located in
a town or a locale named, Captivity; so, Captivity is a
place. At the same time, it is many places. Captivity
can be held in many realms or dimensions. Folks, you
would surely be surprised at what is locked away,
where. Make it make sense? I can't. Witches can hold
a meeting *inside* of a tree. They can lock away your
finances in a rock, in an animal, in your own belly.
Things could be hidden under the sea, beneath the
Earth, on a planet, a star, or an asteroid. None of this

makes sense, this is why we ask the Lord to have His Angels to search for our things, search for our stolen goods, search for our blessings, search for our virtues, and even search for us and the missing parts of our humanity. Those stolen things could be practically anywhere--, except where it is supposed to be. This is the cruel joke occultic people play on the righteous people of God.

Demonic prisons are privately owned and operated; Captivity runs the prison system. In this prison set up they do anything they want--, anything they can get away with. And, they do it as long as a prisoner is there. However, a prisoner can get out. The word, *escape* is in the Bible nearly 60 times, and for good reason.

Our soul is escaped as a bird out of the snare of the fowlers: the snare is broken, and we are escaped. (Psalm 124:7)

Over and again the phrase, *return my captivity* is a plea to God to help, rescue, and deliver the captive. Here, *captivity* is the sentence.

Do not leave my soul in hell, is the cry of the Psalmist.

For thou wilt not leave my soul in hell; neither wilt thou suffer thine Holy One to see corruption. (Psalm 16:10; Acts 2:27)

The above verse is about Jesus and His real trip to Hell, but if Jesus, even though He went willingly--, if Jesus can get caught up in Hell, who do we think we are? We must use that prayer.

The Lord delivered me, from prison, from jail. From Hell. Folks, if David needed deliverance, who do we think we are? Christians still need deliverance.

I sought **the LORD**, and he heard **me**, And **delivered me** from all my fears (Psalm 34:4)

A captive is one taken, as in a war. You may live in a nation of peace right now and praise God for that. For that reason, you may ask, *what war*? A captive is described as one taken in war and most often treated very badly.[a]

What war? The idolatrous captive wasn't waging any war, he was **partying**. The enemy was fully aware there was a conflict going on; the enemy was battling, opposing and oppressing the victim--, many times 24/7. Yet, the captive may have been oblivious to all of that and when captured may ask, What war?

Captivity is the state or period of being held, imprisoned, enslaved, bound, shackled, limited, incarcerated, confined, yoked, in servitude, or in bondage.

In Ephesians 4:8 Jesus led captivity captive. He flipped the script. Captivity is the personality of the condition. Just as a throne is not just the physical seat a monarch would sit upon, it is the aggregation of the

14

powers that create that *throne*. Captivity is a description of a place, a condition, a situation, a time, even a dimension, it is the personality of all of that. Jesus led Captivity captive; Captivity is a person, and he goes about to and fro in the Earth seeking whom he may capture.

Captive

In order to get out of Captivity, one must research to find out how they got there; is this a mistake? Why are they there? At that time, we may simply try to reverse the cause of what got us there. This may include repentance if we find that sin caused the captivity. We may continue begging Mercy and repenting if ancestral sin and inherited iniquity is the cause. Did witchcraft or other occultic curse, cause it? Then we may proceed to break the curse, dismantle the curse, reverse the curse. Reverse the *results* of the curse.

Sadly, some will put up with a curse, if the results aren't too bad. Don't do that. There is always a demon sent to enforce the curse, so, do not allow a curse; the repercussions will get worse and worse, and one demon will invite others, either suddenly, or over time. So, when you first see something is amiss, don't just say something; **pray something.**

So many movies show the prisoner or the accused wanting to or needing to get out of prison to prove their innocence. If your spirit and soul are captive, the only getting out you can do right then is go to the Courts of Heaven. Even against the orders of the prison guards you <u>must</u> seek the Lord. It may not be easy, but you must, you must.

Spiritually one could be guilty of sin and never having committed the transgression. In the natural realm, that is innocent. But in the spiritual realm, God says just *thinking on a woman with lust* **is sin**, for example. Sex is not the only sin that lands a person in Captivity. Sin is a net. This is why there is so much talk of resisting the wiles of an evil woman or a sinful woman in the Proverbs, and other places in the Bible.[b]

How is this resisting to be accomplished when the **knowledge** of sex has already occurred in one's life? A person has already tasted of that Tree that God said don't eat of. When one knows what sex is like and what it feels like, and one likes sex, it is so much harder to resist than if one is still innocent.

Yes, the devil is in this. A person who has never had sex in the natural could have already been attacked and maybe multiple times by sex in the dream. Teenagers even know about this, but do they tell their parents? *Do their parents even ask, "What did you dream last night?"* Without knowledge, the innocent and the sneaky will think they have a secret, and it is a loophole to the transgression in the natural. If they don't know the devil sent this, they may think that they are special, or chosen, or have the best dreams and imagination. Even though they are having sex, they think they'll never get in trouble with their parents.

They won't get pregnant (so they think), or get anyone pregnant in the natural. Of course, they should be worried about more than that, but that is what most people think will catch them or trap them--, pregnancy.

Teach your children at all times.

So, let's continue talking about getting out of Captivity. If someone told you to get a hornet or a bee out of a room that would be hard enough. If someone said, *Kill that fly*, that may be doable, but harder. If someone said, *There's a mosquito in here, we have got to kill it--*, that is more difficult, still because of the size and the zig zaggy-wilyness of the mosquito.

Next, we are down to a fruit fly, it is landing all over the fruit bowl on the table and possibly laying eggs. It is disgusting, so it has to go. **Can you even see it?** Can you find it to get rid of it? Smaller than that are the no-see-ums, flies of the Ceratopogonidae family. They are so small you can't see them, but they bite.

Spiritual things are even harder than that to deal with unless you have spiritual vision, else they are completely invisible. Without dealing with what has been "created" in the spirit in one's youth, by the time one is an adult, even a young adult, there is so much opposing them, and they can't see it, don't know it, and they have a lot to fight. By age 40, if not dealt with spiritually—wow! It could be overwhelming.

> But I keep under my body, and bring it
> into subjection: lest that by any means, when I have
> preached to others, I myself should be a castaway.
> (1 Corinthians 9:27)

I bring my body under. That should include bringing your emotions under. That should include bringing your desires under. A person can be captive by feelings, urges, drives, cravings, yearnings. *I feel like* is the feeling and sometimes the words right before many sins are committed. The very sins that make a man or woman a captive.

Captivity can be by many means:

- Captive by emotions, memories, and emotional pain, such as over -grieving, and evil soul ties.
- Captive by your physical body, flesh, sex, pain
- Captive by *things and stuff* such as money, cars, houses.
- Spiritually captive by pride, jealousy, hatred, resentment, guilt

Once you are captive you could become a devil agent. The devil just flips a switch, and you are his puppet. As Captivity is a person, your name becomes **Captive** if you are caught by him, then at that time he **owns you**, or certainly believes that he owns you.

Feelings? Jesus says He stands at the door and knocks. Peculiar to Jesus, He does use the door.

The devil, however, stands anywhere and knocks anywhere and everywhere. He tries anything and everything until something hits. You get a feeling in your body somewhere that sparks you to want to do something that you may call *fun*, but it may be ungodly, not expedient, rebellious, stupid, or destructive.

That's the devil knocking.

Your tongue finds the roof of your mouth, your salivary glands secrete saliva as if you are having something sour--, that idea has been introduced into your mind. You want something sour? Hmm, what will it be? Sour candy? Lemonade? Key Lime pie? A margarita? Where did you suddenly get that idea or craving? I mean, it's 9:00 am in the morning and this is what you're thinking about? You are captive already, or the devil is **knocking. Don't answer, he is trying to get you to open the door so he can come into your life and** make you into a captive.

Oh, some will argue that it is their body telling them what it needs. The body is the only part of you that can wear out and rust and die, WHY would you let that part of you run the most precious parts of you, your spirit and your soul? Your spirit and soul are divine; the body is flesh. Your spirit and soul are eternal; the body is mortal. Your spirit and soul have been here a long, long time – that flesh of yours is the new kid on the block. So, you are going to let your child run the "grown ups"—your spirit and soul and affect their eternal destination?

Is that wise?

So, to put your flesh in charge of your life, destiny, and eternal destination is like letting a foreign government decide who should be the president of your country of residence. The devil is the foreign government. There is nothing good in any flesh.

You get a little tingle, or feel a little heat or a little rise *down there* and you believe you want sex. *Do you?* Whose idea was that? Is the purpose of this sex to procreate? Is it to show love to your spouse? Or is it because you just want to get *busy*? Are you even thinking of your spouse, or are you being pointed to anyone who is available? The devil is knocking. Don't answer. If you feel you **MUST** answer, you are captive.

Jesus comes in through the door. The devil knocks **anywhere** and everywhere to see if you will bite, jump, answer. It is to make you captive, or you are already a captive and he wants to keep you that way by putting sin opportunities before your eyes. The devil has no respect for you, whatsoever; he is not throwing gifts your way, those are traps, and you are his slave.

That *tingle*? Maybe it's just pressure on your bladder and you need to go to the restroom. This is not about sex at all, but *something* is making you think it is. Resist.

What you know is right, what you know to do and don't do that, but instead you are what the world calls and celebrates as being fun and *spontaneous* – you are captive. The spontaneity demon is at work. You are not to be congratulated, you need deliverance. Do what the Word says, do what God says, not any whimsical thing. Laws and rules are for your protection; follow them.

You may complain, saying something like, *"This is going wrong, that doesn't work, this disappoints me all the time--, can't I have just <u>one</u> or <u>**two**</u> simple pleasures? I deserve this guilty pleasure."* Pleasures of sin are for but a moment, but the iniquity and captivity can last a lifetime. Captivity can last **more** than one lifetime. If the devil has you in captivity it is because he is planning that your eternal destination is Hell; he has put a claim on you.

You must get out!

Don't just accept it and say something religious like, *in the sweet by and by, all my problems will fall away.*

Will they? And, how?

You'd better work while it is day because the night comes when no man can work. Get into spiritual warfare, fasting, praying, reading the Word, listening to deliverance preaching, praise and worship, whatever it takes to get out of the claws of Captivity and the clauses of evil covenants.

Saints of God. I'm talking to you and I'm talking also to myself, being a first partaker of all the Lord is teaching by His Spirit.

A Living Hell

This person (your jailer/tormentor) makes one's life a living hell. We blame that on people, but it's the devil behind the curtain who has programmed hell into a life. Your natural life mirrors your spiritual life.

Your kingdom come, your will be done, on earth as it is in heaven, (Matthew 6:10 NIV)

The Word of God is sharper than a two-edged sword, but it is especially grievous when the devil is misusing it against man with his three-pronged pitchfork. Let it be done on Earth as it is in Heaven is the Christian's hope and vision of life here, that the wonderful things that happen in the Third Heaven will flow into the natural for our abundance and enjoyment, for our life and godliness.

Well, there's the devil. Things that happen in heavenly places can include the second heaven, where the seat of Satan is. Unfortunately, if we are not discerning and discriminating, and upright before the Lord, what is proclaimed in hellish places like the second heaven can also follow that Word. Things that happen in the natural happen in the spiritual realm first. It is at that time that we can agree or disagree with that spiritual thing. If we do nothing, the hellish thing will come. If we do nothing even about a good prophetic Word, it still may not come to pass because there is the second heaven blocking, twisting, turning the blessings of God to steal from mankind and also to torment him.

We allow or disallow by binding and loosing. Binding and *loosing* is given to us by our authority in Christ Jesus. The problem is, we bind and *loose* all day and all night. But how are we binding and what are we *loosing*? It is not only the things we say, although what we say is important, but it is also things we do.

Folks fail to see several things: What a sin is. That there are consequences to sin. Can't love the world. Can't do what the world is doing. What you do at night, in your sleep can also be a sin and accounted to you. Your dream life tells the story of your awake life; sometimes it forecasts your awake life. Night dreams are not always literal—only true prophets see literal night visions. All others must interpret their dreams, as we dream in symbols.

Similarly, your awake life directs your dream life. Your dream life is your spiritual life. Let it be done on Earth as it is in Heaven--- think this: in heavenly realms. The second heaven where the seat of Satan *is,* is a heavenly realm—it's landscape however is hell, prison, Captivity.

Experiencing a living hell here on Earth? You are alive on Earth, but in hell, in some other dimension—even in heavenly places, second heavenly places, at the same time.

Your spirit life directs your physical life at the same time your physical life can direct your spirit life. Your physical life must be all into Christ to do this. Your physical life must be willfully godlike, obedient, and faithful, to properly direct your spirit man.

Every night as you are sleeping, your spirit man can go out into spiritual realms. Is he doing things of his own volition? Or is he being called out, summoned, and controlled? When we are absent the body, then shouldn't we be with the LORD? Are we? Where are we at night? What spiritual realms are we visiting?

Captivity by Hell is something like a work-at-night, and then be released in the daytime program. You've heard some people say that – they are working night and day. Do they realize that what they have said as an exaggeration may be the very truth? Whether they know what they said or not, if they are captured, they are.

Go to bed tired, wake up tired. You are working all night. At night you wish it was day. In the morning you wish it was night --- you are captive, and suffering under the Curse of the Law.

In the morning thou shalt say, Would God it were
even! and at even thou shalt say, Would God it were
morning! for the fear of thine heart wherewith thou
shalt fear, and for the sight of thine eyes which thou
shalt see. (Deuteronomy 28:67)

Besides the evil of this prison, there is spiritual
power running it. If you do not have any spiritual
power to counteract it; then you are helpless and must
do as they say. Your only hope is to have more power,
position, authority, and higher connections and
willingness in the daytime to use it and awareness
when you are in spiritual realms, as in the sleep to use
your authority. That is your way out.

And, with all of that, you must be bold and
courageous. You must not fear because what you shall
see with your eyes may bring fear upon you.
(Deuteronomy 28:67)

How do you get out? Simply walk out?
Escape? Get broken out? It will take Jesus; it will take
deliverance to get out of Captivity.

Captivity to Captivity

And when he cometh, he shall smite the land of Egypt, *and deliver* such *as are* for death to death; and such *as are* for **captivity** to **captivity**; and such *as are* for the sword to the sword. (Jeremiah 43:11)

Bondages and yokes. Ancestral chains. The devil has certain families, and he knows it. It is a done deal. Have you noticed some families, from the poor to the very rich, anywhere in the world but their lives are disastrous and miserable, full of turmoil, weirdness, and possibly even early death?

Devil deals have been made. They may have at birth already belonged to the devil, lock, stock, and barrel. They are not just meant for captivity, they are born into captivity and have no choice – well, nearly no choice. If the Word is preached to them, if Jesus is introduced to them, they now have a choice.

Have you noticed families where one someone gets away and renounces the family name, or the family brand, or the family money, especially? They want nothing to do with that family and would rather starve than take family finances?

That person has declared a fast, of sorts… and is trying desperately to break away in the <u>natural</u> from their family. They must break away spiritually also, or at best, at first, but this is a start, and it may be all they know, really.

This works two ways; a child can rebel from a righteous family to embark upon stupid and perilous paths, as with the Prodigal son.

Captured in a vicious cycle of poverty and loss, and misery and disappointment? You may see it in the collective--, in your entire family or bloodline, but since it is in *your* bloodline you may think this is normal. It is "normal" for your bloodline, but is it normal for the rest of the world? Is it normal for the rest of the saved world? Is it normal when compared to the Word of God?

I am not calling anyone an animal, but animals bred in captivity have little to no idea that they are in captivity. Further, they would not be able to survive if released into the wild after having been reared domestically. Can your pet dog or cat survive on the streets after you have provided everything for them since they were first weaned? Probably not.

So, the problem is we get used to captivity and may adapt a, *well-that's-the-way-it-is* attitude.

Some people are made for captivity – some are made for the day of evil. You've heard folks say, "*That boy just won't do right.*" If you have seriously prayed for *that boy* but he can't seem to be set free from his evil tendencies and bondages, perhaps he was seriously evil dedicated or he was made for the evil day. Only God knows that. If you pray, especially if you are an intercessor, prayer warrior or prophet, God will tell you. If *that boy* is in Captivity, keep praying for him, unless God tells you otherwise.

When I shall bring
again their captivity, the captivity of Sodom and her daughters, and the captivity of Samaria and her daughters, then *will I bring again* the captivity of thy captives in the midst of them: (Ezekiel 16:53)

And say unto the Ammonites, Hear the word of the Lord GOD; Thus saith the Lord GOD; Because thou saidst, Aha, against my sanctuary, when it was profaned; and against the land of Israel, when it was desolate; and against the house of Judah, when they went into captivity; (Ezekiel 25:3)

I share these Scriptures to show you how many times a people, or a person may go into captivity, over and over, based on who they are, their bloodline, their behavior, their lack of repentance, stony heart, evil heart--, their nature. The prophets have to often speak harsh things that people, especially those with evil hearts do not want to hear. Worse, if they are already in captivity, it is very difficult for them to even hear what *thus saith the Lord.* It is why ungodly people hate the prophets, as well they are either ignorant of, or hate the Word of God.

The young men of Aven and of Pibeseth shall fall by the sword: and these *cities* shall go into captivity. At Tehaphnehes also the day shall be darkened, when I shall break there the yokes of

Egypt: and the pomp of her strength shall cease in her: as for her, a cloud shall cover her, and her daughters shall go into captivity. (Ezekiel 30: 17-18)

Many times, in my professional capacity as a dentist, I ask people who seem to already be unsettled before the procedure even starts, *"Do you want me to tell you what I'm going to do, or just do it?"* God is far more merciful than any human, me included. **He tells people what He is going to do.** The more He tells you, and especially the more advance notice you get, the more you can have opportunity to repent, to change, to prepare, or decide to go along with what God just told you He would do. I try my best to do exactly as I say I will do regarding people and their dental care. I also give people the choice to proceed or stop; I force no one to do anything.

God is different than humans in that His Word has already preceded Him and what His Word says is what He does. It is what must happen. Graciously he reminds humans that this is the consequence of what you chose to do, and often, have already done. Now, this is what will happen because of that. In this way, God is really giving you an opportunity to choose twice. You chose life or death already. You chose to sin. Now you can choose to repent, do nothing, or even double down on your sin. Repenting is your choice to stop--, stopping both your own misbehavior, and asking God to be more merciful and remove the iniquity and stop the punishment.

But His Word is forever settled; He is just sending notice by the prophet of what, and also when. Don't blame the messenger. Don't get rid of the prophet, if you are the problem, God by His Mercy sent you a warning. The prophet obeyed God. If you are nose blind to your own sins, then you will blame anyone, even the prophet of God.

O Jerusalem, Jerusalem, thou
that killest the prophets, and stonest them which are sent unto thee, how often would I have gathered thy children. (Matthew 23:37)

Jesus Led Captivity Captive

Wherefore he saith, When he ascended up on high, he led captivity captive, and gave gifts unto men. (Ephesians 4:8)

Jesus led Captivity captive. Jesus took Captivity captive. Jesus took the keys. Wardens are known to have a lot of keys because they have a lot of cells. Jesus took the keys To Hell, Death, and the Grave.

Captivity is the state of being a prisoner. It is being in the power of an enemy by force, control, violence, or the threat of it. Captivity is a state of being under control, in subjection; servitude; slavery.

Everybody says they don't want to be controlled, but do their actions reflect what they say? If getting a certain amount of money every month, not for a needful period in your life, but *for* life, requires you to be a certain way, act a certain way, do this, but don't do that--, is that not captivity? But you're getting money you may try to justify – yeah, money is the jailer. That is captivity; money is controlling the person.

But, we've been redeemed from Captivity – but we have to accept it, we have to lean in and appropriate it. Not only that, we have to avoid future and repeated, as well as eternal captivity. You hear so many people say they want to make Heaven. Well, good. Why not live free on your way to Heaven? **To lead *Captivity* captive, in Scripture, means to subdue those who have held you (or others) in slavery, or *captivity.*** (Psalms 98:1)

Saints of God, because Jesus took Captivity captive, and we are *in Him*, we have a certain authority ourselves. We have that same authority.

Casting down imaginations, and every high
thing that exalteth itself against the knowledge of
God, and bringing
into **captivity** every thought to the obedience of
Christ; (2 Corinthians 10:5)

All our thoughts come from somewhere. We are vessels, so all of our thoughts, good or bad, come from outside of us. We think we are thinking our own thoughts, but these influences are either from God, or not from God. When an influence, thought, or idea comes that is not from God then we take it captive – like Jesus. This means that the *spirit* that gave the idea or the impulse is taken captive. Binding and *loosing* – yes, you're a prison guard as well, one who should possess the gates of your enemies. But when we fail to do this, anything goes. The devil is a default authority on Earth; we have to **invite** the Lord, but we don't have to invite the devil, although some do. The devil is around, the prince of this world. The prince of the powers of the air, and so many names that let you know his location, authority, and likely antics.

But Jesus descended and took Captivity captive. As mentioned, that means to take captive what has been holding you as a captive. That is to turn the tables on the jailer and now you take control and authority over what had been controlling or dominating you. Jesus did this for mankind. Listed below are those whom the Son set free by virtue of His descent and Ascension.

- Old Testament saints. Some believe that Jesus freed the Old Testament saints who died before Christ's atonement, and took them with Him into Glory when He ascended.

- Souls of believers. Jesus led the souls of believers who died before He came from Sheol into Paradise. This gave them the freedom of life with God.
- People in bondage. Jesus came to free people who were in bondage and couldn't escape on their own.
- People held captive. Jesus came to tell people who were held captive that they could be set free.

Jesus' work on Calvary and His resurrection conquered death, not just at that moment, but looking at the list, Jesus worked in and out of Time, setting people from the past, present and future (that's us) free from Captivity, bondage and the yokes of sin.

That's still us. Shall we not receive it? Shall we not appropriate this amazing deliverance?

Wherefore he saith, When he ascended up on high, he led captivity captive, and gave gifts unto men. (Now that he ascended, what is it but that he also descended first into the lower parts of the earth? He that descended is the same also that ascended up far above all heavens, that he might fill all things. (Ephesians 4:7-10)

The expression, *to take captivity captive* means to flip the script on one's bondage, imprisonment, or captivity. Jesus, who knew no sin became sin for us. So, if Jesus knew no sin, then He could never have been captive or imprisoned. This could be the main reason why the Pharisees and Sadducees kept trying to find reasons to lay hands on Him and imprison Him, or even put Him to death, but they never could.

They never could, until He:

- **Became sin** for us. Now that He has become sin, then the curses that go with sin and its iniquity apply.
- Willingly became sin and willingly laid down His life.

No man taketh it from me, but I lay it down of myself. I have power to lay it down, and I have power to take it again. This commandment have I received of my Father. (John 10:18)

But at that time, that is not what they thought. Like the devil who influenced them, they thought, *"We finally got Him."* I reflect back to you, Pharisees and Sadducees, and whatever they are called in our times, could never have believed that they, themselves were the problem. No, to them, Jesus was the problem, and His followers too. Their campaign was not one of deliverance for themselves – there was nothing wrong with them, surely. Their campaign was one of riddance, to get rid of this guy with the new doctrine and had crowds following Him, and healing people— even on the Sabbath. After Jesus, then they endeavored to get rid of the rest of them, as well.

Jesus came to help them--; He came to help all of mankind, but they wanted to get rid of the Help because, as far as they were concerned, as far as they could *see*, there was nothing wrong with them, nothing wrong with the world they lived in and nothing wrong with anything – since they were rich and in charge. Yet, they were captive and could not *see*, nor could they see that they were captive; they were wretched and blind. They were captive to the world, and therefore beholden to the prince of this world, their status, their positions, their wealth and perceived importance. They were captive y the devil—the same devil who took Jesus up on a high place and offered

Him the same things the Pharisees obviously had accepted and become captivated with, and *captive* by.

They needed deliverance and Jesus was the only one who could set them free.

He still can; and still does, for the living. Jesus' work on Calvary transcends Time, as well as every realm and dimension. That means that wherever you are captive, wherever you (your spirit) are being held captive, Jesus can free you. Whenever you became captive, Jesus can free you. If you sinned, and all of us have, and that made you captive for the very first time, Jesus can free you. If you became captive 500 years ago, in another timeline or dimension, because of the sins and iniquity of your ancestors, but now you know better, Jesus can free you.

Thou hast ascended on high, thou hast
led **captivity** captive: thou hast received gifts for
men; yea, *for* the rebellious also, that the
LORD God might dwell *among them.* (Psalm 68:18)

You have got to know it, want it, ask for it, receive it. If it just could happen without any work or effort on your part, you would not be captive; no one in your bloodline would be captive or would ever have been captive.

Furnish Thyself

No one just randomly lands in spiritual prison, in captivity. There is a whole legal process in the spirit before this can happen. God gives you notice and plenty of time to address the matter, as well as time to repent and avoid this captivity.

> O thou daughter dwelling in Egypt, furnish thyself to go into **captivity**: for Noph shall be waste and desolate without an inhabitant. (Jeremiah 46:19)

God says that He does nothing in the Earth without first revealing it to His prophets. The above verse from Jeremiah informs the *daughter* dwelling in Egypt to get ready, pack your bags, you're going into captivity. Well, if you have good sense you may want to talk to God, or at least ask the Prophet, *Why? When? What did I do? What do I need to repent for? Is it too late to repent right now?* But man has either a devilish or foolish way about himself, Man may already know what he did and thinks he has gotten away with it, or can still get away with it by feigning innocence. He may stubbornly refuse to repent, as if he can box with God. He may be nose blind to his own sinful ways. You see where this is going, right? God probably gave more than one warning and man dismissed them all, until God couldn't do anything else for him; the Law must be fulfilled. The Word of God must and will perform.

Let's look at Bible precedence:

Captivity of the Israelites was foretold more than once.

> I will scatter you among the nations and will draw out my sword and pursue you. Your land will be laid waste, and your cities will lie in ruins.
> (Leviticus 26:33)

> The Lord shall bring thee, and thy king which thou shalt set over thee, unto a nation which neither thou nor thy fathers have known; and there shalt thou serve other gods, wood and stone.
> (Deuteronomy 28:36).

Did they listen? Folks hate a prophet that is not a game show host giving out cars, money, and exotic vacations. Instead of heeding the Word from the Lord, many will disparage the Prophet and shut him down.

> O Jerusalem, Jerusalem, thou that killest the prophets, and stonest them which are sent unto thee, how often would I have gathered thy children together, even as a hen gathereth her chickens under her wings, and ye would not! (Matthew 23:37)

Are we still doing that? When a voice tells us something we do not want to hear, do we disregard the person speaking and believe that the prophetic word is from them alone and will go away when they go away. That is still the ministry of riddance. Have we not learned that doesn't work when that mouthpiece is of God, and that Word is God's Word?

Captivity of the 10 Tribes was foretold three times. First, in 2 Kings 17:6. Then again in 2 Kings 17:23-24, and a third time in 2 Kings 18:9-12. And, it surely came to pass. The Word of the Lord does not return to Him void, but it will accomplish what He says it will accomplish.

There are many other examples of God sending His Word through a prophet, but the people collectively, essentially dismissed the opportunity to repent and turn from their wicked ways so that the Lord would not even allow the captivity. Oh, it is so much easier to never go into captivity than to try to get out of it.

Captivity is allowed when there is judgment on a people, a land, a bloodline, a tribe, or a nation. Folks, God is not playing, but if you are reading this book, you are already the type who knows that to be true.

But after that our fathers had provoked the God of heaven unto wrath, he gave them into the hand of Nebuchadnezzar the king of Babylon, the Chaldean, who destroyed this house, and carried the people away into Babylon. (Ezra 5:12)

Therefore my people are gone into captivity, because they have no knowledge: and their honourable men are famished, and their multitude dried up with thirst. (Isaiah 5:13)

Thus saith the Lord of hosts; Behold, I will send upon them the sword, the famine, and the pestilence, and will make them like vile figs, that cannot be eaten, they are so evil.

And I will persecute them with the sword, with the famine, and with the pestilence, and will deliver them to be removed to all the kingdoms of the earth, to be a curse, and an astonishment, and an hissing, and a reproach, among all the nations whither I have driven them:

Because they have not hearkened to my words, saith the Lord, which I sent unto them by my servants the prophets, rising up early and sending them; but ye would not hear, saith the Lord. (Jeremiah 29:17-19)[c]

I will make boys their leaders, and toddlers their rulers. (Isaiah 3:4 NLT)

Bible Precedence

The captivity of the nation of Israel began when the kingdom of the ten tribes was invaded over and again by Assyrian kings. These invading kings imposed tribute of Israel.[d] The Tribes were taken captive and were carried away along with the inhabitants of Galilee into Assyria.[e]

Samaria was seized and a great number of people were transported to Assyria which ended the kingdom of the ten tribes. [f]

In 605 B.C., Nebuchadnezzar and his army came into Jerusalem took the city as well as Jewish captives. This was called the "seventy years" captivity (Daniel 9:1-2)

Nebuchadnezzar, in 2 Kings 24 invaded Jerusalem a second time and killed King Jehoiakim, placing his son, Jehoiachin on the throne. [g]

The Bible historians say that Jehoiachin was 18 years old when he was made king. Again:

I will make boys their leaders, and toddlers their rulers. (Isaiah 3:4 NLT)

Jehoiachin was not the youngest to ever become king. Josiah was only 8 years old, but his ways pleased the Lord. (2 Chronicles 34). But a youthful and ignorant leader, or king further destabilizes the country.

Jehoiachin only ruled for three months; before Nebuchadnezzar invaded Jerusalem a **third time.** This time they took even more Jews to Babylon as captives--, upward of 10,000.[h] Among them was the young king Jehoiachin, his mother, all his princes and officers, and the prophet, Ezekiel.

Nebuchadnezzar also took all their *stuff*, their treasures and things of value as spoils of war and desecrated their synagogue, their place of worship.

Zedekiah (Mattaniah, who was king at that time) became a prisoner in Babylon at the hands of Nebuchadnezzar. His eyes were put out, and he was kept in close confinement till his death, (2 Kings 25:7) Everything of value was taken and then the city was burned. The city walls were levelled to the ground around 586 BC. Only a few of the poorest people remained, left there to till the ground and dress the vineyards. The rest, the best and the brightest were carried away captives to Babylon. This was the third and last deportation of Jews into the Babylonish captivity.

Saints of God, take note, that a city or a nation can be under captivity and still have a "king." Whether it is a good king, a godly king or not determines if that captivity will hold.

Do we not also have a King? Our God is the King of kings. People say that a Christian cannot have demons or need deliverance. **A city, a nation, or an individual can have a king and still be captive.** Christians have a King, yet they can still become captives and still need deliverance.

David was a man after God's own heart, yet he sinned with Bathsheba and had Uriah essentially murdered. The Prophet Nathan had to come to him to set him straight. Folks, the Word of God when it is received is deliverance---, we go to church to get that every Sunday, and sometimes on Wednesday night Bible Study. Peter was a whole Disciple of Jesus and in anger cut off a soldier's ear. Then Peter lied three times that he didn't even know Jesus all in the same night. What made Peter do these things? He needed correction. Correction is deliverance.

We must call on our King for our deliverance. Amen.

Meanwhile, back in Babylon, In the first year of his reign, around 536 B.C., Cyrus issued a decree liberating the Jewish captives, and permitted them to return to Jerusalem and rebuild the city and the temple.[i] Around 43,000 came out of captivity, (Ezra 2:64-65), and 50% more who were both male and female servants.

Later, other Jews of the Babylonish captivity returned to Jerusalem under both Ezra and Nehemiah. Oddly, more people remained in the land to which they had been carried, than came out when they were given permission to leave. They became known as the Jews of the "dispersion" (John 7:35; 1 Peter 1:1). The number of exiles that chose to remain was probably about six times the number of those who returned.

Collective captivity.

Folks, seems nearly 300,000 "former" captives preferred to stay in the land of their captivity. Some people learn to like captivity. They liked their captor and oppressor? Some like slavery. Some don't like change. Some don't think for themselves any longer.

We need Jesus.

We must remember what got them captive in the first place: idolatry.

Idolatry is like a speed trap in the natural. You know where the cops are hidden, you know you're speeding or breaking the law in some way, but somehow those cops can sit at the same location day after day and still catch speeders. They aren't just ticketing out of towners, but also locals can still get stopped and ticketed by traffic cops.

That is because humans keep doing the same thing over and over again. Many times, it is the same humans doing the same thing, repeatedly.

And the children of Dan set up the graven image: and Jonathan, the son of Gershom, the son of Manasseh, he and his sons were priests to the tribe of Dan until the day of the **captivity** of the land. (Judges 18:30)

The first thing that happens in the natural to a speeder is they are charged a fine, that is called *tribute* in the Bible. After that, the Law may charge you more or take something from you. they may keep you away from your car or driving for a while. They may keep you from **people** for a while, separating you – putting you in Captivity (jail). All this is punitive and designed to teach you a lesson and instill some behavior modification in you.

It doesn't always work. Man is a creature of habit and habits can be hard to break. The cops know this so they sit in the same place over and again and catch speeders – even the same speeders. This tells us that those who don't learn go from captivity to captivity, even if they get out for a while in between each jailing. We have heard of people who are just like that in the natural. Recidivism is real, it is the tendency of a convicted criminal or sinner to repeat his crime or sin.

Jews kept sinning, as humans do. And they kept repeating the sin of idolatry, which God hates.

Judah is gone into **captivity** because of affliction, and because of great servitude: she dwelleth among the heathen, she findeth no rest: all her persecutors overtook her between the straits.
(Lamentations 1:3)

This is where a spiritual speed bump would well behoove us. Those of us who are teachable will learn.

Ways Into Captivity

Sin.

- Your own sin.
- The sins of the parents, ancestors.
- Any sin. Repeated sin.
- Unrepented sin.
- Sins of omission.
- Sins of commission.
- Sins of the mind.
- Transgressions.
- Bloodline iniquity.

I hear so many folks finally admit the thing they should have led with when seeking deliverance. Casually, in passing they may say that their mother was a witch. *What?* That's huge. They may finally share that some other relative practiced New Ageism or was a Wiccan, or had a lot of crystals. Saints of God, if your parent, either parent was a witch, then you are a witch/warlock. You are born into it. Markers are in your blood for that. You must renounce witchcraft and every evil dedication. You are born already in captivity. The devil has already claimed you; now you've got to get away from him and be **all in Christ.**

Other sure ways into Captivity is unforgiveness, seeking vengeance, eye for an eye--. Live by the sword, die by the sword. Live by Captivity, die by it. When you think about it, witchcraft is all of the aforementioned; could be why God hates it so much.

This prayer is from Kitty Cleveland on renouncing the occult.

"Heavenly Father, in the name of your only begotten Son, Jesus Christ, I renounce Satan and all his works, all forms of witchcraft, the use of divination, the practice of sorcery, dealing with mediums, channeling with spirit guides, the Ouija board, tarot cards, astrology, Reiki, hypnosis, automatic writing, horoscopes, numerology, the Enneagram, all types of fortune telling, palm readings, New Age spirituality, and anything else associated with the occult or Satan.

"In the name of Jesus Christ who came in the flesh, and by the power of his Cross, his Precious Blood, and his Resurrection, I renounce and forsake my involvement in all of them, and I choose you alone, Lord Jesus.

"I confess all these sins before you and ask you to cleanse and forgive me for my divided heart. I ask you, Lord Jesus, to come into my heart, give me your merciful love, and make me holy. I ask you to send forth your Holy Spirit to baptize me with love, just as you baptized your disciples on the day of Pentecost.

"I thank you, Heavenly Father, for strengthening my inner spirit with the power of your Holy Spirit, so that Christ may dwell in my heart. Through faith, rooted and grounded in love, may I be able to comprehend with all the saints, the breadth, length, height and depth of Christ's love which surpasses all understanding. Amen!"

https://kittycleveland.com/prayer-to-renounce-the-occult/

Other less brazen and perhaps less obvious ways into Captivity include, doublemindedness, and hypocrisy.

And shall cut him asunder, and appoint him his portion with the hypocrites: there shall be weeping and gnashing of teeth (Matthew 24:51)

Also, being lazy and not working at all. And, especially not working toward destiny and doing the work and the will of the Lord who sent you here in the first place.

And cast ye the unprofitable servant into outer darkness: there shall be weeping and gnashing of teeth. (Matthew 25:30)

A Long Time

In 2 Kings 24:15, Jehoiachin, his mother, wives and officers were carried away to Babylon. They were placed in Captivity, which lasted 250 years. Folks, how many of us have that kind of time to dilly dally about in Captivity? That's not only a person's entire life, but it may also be as many as four generations of a family. Many would be in Captivity all of their lives.

Can we all consider this when we **decide** to sin?

Unless God is merciful, and we repent quickly we will definitely see some fallout from the iniquity of sin. **Can we also think that we are writing the program for our children's lives as well?** After all if we are in Captivity, they will be born into Captivity. How will they get out? Like, *ever*?

I've shared earlier that animals who are bred in Captivity have NO IDEA that they are in Captivity. So how will they figure out that they are in Captivity, and that they need to get out, or how to get out?

Worst of all, if they get out, can they make it in the world that is outside of Captivity?

Lord, have Mercy –, this thing just really hit me.

And it came to pass in the seven and thirtieth year of the **captivity** of Jehoiachin king of Judah, in the twelfth month, on the seven and twentieth *day* of the month, *that* Evilmerodach king of Babylon in the year that he began to reign did lift up the head of Jehoiachin king of Judah out of prison;
(2 Kings 25:27)

The above verse reads, *In the 37th year of the captivity.* In the natural, most people would freak out if they had to be in jail overnight for whatever reason. The 37th year! And the chief jailer was named Evilmerodach. Folks, if the word evil is in front of a name and there isn't even a hyphen, the prisoners are in a world of hurt. So, in the natural most couldn't bear a prison like that. If they had known, they'd have been scared straight.

Then I came to them of the captivity at Telabib, that dwelt by the river of Chebar, and I sat where they sat, and remained there astonished among them seven days. (Ezekiel 3:15)

Why sit in a spiritual prison? It will be far worse than one in the natural realm. In the spirit—in spiritual jail or prison, the conditions are horrendous. We should never become acclimated and then just stay there and just take it. As if this is our lot in life?

Of course, not.

Born and bred in captivity, or stuck in it for so long, without the Word of God the captive will not know that there is something better for him.

The Hebrews were slaves in Egypt for 430 years. Captivity may last a long, long time—generations. Captivity could be the result of being captured by the devil, or a punishment for unrepentant, chronic sin. The warnings are both in the Bible, and out of the mouth of the Prophet. The consequences are dire, so why do we repeat sin? Sin has bondage. Sin has yokes, that's why it is addictive and so repetitive.

Sin is anointed. There is an evil anointing to sin; it is with the devil who is presenting the sin-idea to you. It pulls you or draws you, attracts you, entices you. You should be resisting, but is your ability to resist stronger than their ability to entice you to sin? It's a **war of anointings**--, is the evil anointing stronger than the anointing that you have along with the anointing and sure connection of the one you are connected to, Jesus Christ?

It depends.

It does not depend on whether God has power or not. God is the greatest power; all power belongs to God. It does not depend on whether God wants to bless you and help you, because He does. But the anointing of God is available to you only if you are in Christ. It depends on how much you are in Christ and single-mindedly practicing the disciplines of the faith. You cannot be double-minded.

It depends on YOU and how much worship you've given it. The more worship, time, attention, and sacrifices, including money and things of value you've given the Darkside, the stronger that anointing will be to pull on you, to draw you into whatever sin they are sponsoring. You create the magnet that draws to you the thing that matches it. Look on sin, think on sin, worship sin, go to sinful places, do sinful things, then <u>you</u> have really invited the sin that is inviting you to more sin. **Sin invites sin.**

SIN IS WORSHIP. HOLINESS IS WORSHIP. Which are you doing? Whom are you worshipping? Are you double-minded and trying to do both?

Your ability to resist the anointing that is on sin depends on <u>you</u>. You can pray, God don't let me sin all you want, but you have to have done the work to build up your spirit man to resist prior to the presentation of the *sinvitation*. Your soul should be well-ordered, prospered, else there will be openings in your soul for the sinvitation to invite you to sin. The prayers of the righteous avails much. Much what? Much power, much anointing. So prior to the sin attack, you have to have already prepared yourself. Stay prayed up, saints of God.

If you lose, you sin. If you sin, you get captured. Worse than that, you can continue to sin while you are in Captivity, prison, jail or lockdown—that is to ensure that you will stay there.

It is possible to spend one's entire youth in captivity, and I don't just mean *juvie*. A guilty person in jail, prison, or lockdown in the natural is already a captive in the spirit. Imprisonment in the natural is the manifestation of what is happening spiritually to that person. As we know, everyone in jail is not guilty. Recall, Joseph was in jail, but he was innocent.

Why do so many imprisoned men *find* Islam? Is the Islamic leader in jail also? Why ae his followers in jail? He certainly is not the one who can get them out. **Jesus is the only way out of Captivity**. Say what you will, more than one person who has had a near death experience and saw the other side have seen their fearless, mortal leader in Hell. Captivity is Hell. Jail is Hell.

I am He that liveth, and was dead; and behold, I am alive for evermore, Amen, and have the keys of hell and of death. (Revelations 1:8)

Jesus is the only way to the Father. Jesus is the only way to Salvation and redemption. Jesus is the only way out of Captivity in the spirit and in the natural. Jesus has the keys to Death, Hell, and the Grave. Jesus took Captivity captive, no one else.

Wherefore he saith, When he ascended up on high,
he led captivity captive, and gave gifts unto men.
(Ephesians 4:8)

It is possible to spend an entire marriage in
Captivity--, and misery. One spouse is waiting, fasting
and praying for their spouse to come in off the street –
but the roving spouse is addicted to and in bondage to
sin and the streets; they are captive. At least one of
them didn't know that one or both of them were in
Captivity when they agreed to the marriage. It is
impossible to love God with all of you, if part of you
is in Captivity. It is impossible to love your spouse
with your whole heart, if part of you is in Captivity.
The street-loving spouse may not even want to be in
the street, but the power over him, the dark anointing
that says cheat on your spouse, or your legs can never
stay home is making him. **Captivity** is forcing them to
be a horrible spouse.

It is possible to spend one's <u>entire life</u> in
Captivity. Destiny is down the drain because a person
may have rejected knowledge and hated instruction,
did not observe the fear of the Lord. It depends on
your sentence. My God of Mercy!

When we have grieved God but by His Mercy,
He hasn't turned us over to death He may not be able
to help us if we haven't repented and turned back to
Him. Therefore, we may end up in a spiritual gulag or
dungeon.

For therefore he sent unto
us *in* Babylon, saying, This ***captivity*** *is* long: build ye
houses, and dwell *in them*, and plant gardens, and
eat the fruit of them. (Jeremiah 29:28)

My God of Mercy! We have gone from, *furnish
yourself,* that is pack your bags, to now furnish your
house because you are going to be living here.
Captivity is a town, city or suburb where none of us
should want to live.

And thou, Pashur, and all that dwell in thine
house shall go into **captivity**: and thou shalt come to
Babylon, and there thou shalt die, and shalt be
buried there, thou, and all thy friends, to whom
thou hast prophesied lies. (Jeremiah 20:6)

Oh, saints of God, here is another sin aside
from speeding and sex sins. It is propha-lying. Careful
of calling yourself a prophet. Careful of saying that
God said a thing. Captivity awaits the prophets who lie
in the Name of the Lord. The Ten Commandments
forbid us to lie on one another; we are not to even bear
false witness against our neighbor. Shall we then
decide to lie on God?

Lord, forbid!

Send to all them of the **captivity**, saying, Thus
saith the LORD concerning Shemaiah the
Nehelamite; Because that Shemaiah hath
prophesied unto you, and I sent him not, and he
caused you to trust in a lie: (Jeremiah 29:31)

Individuals

Sin is the way into Captivity.

But I see another law in my members, warring
against the law of
my mind, and bringing me into **captivity** to the
law of sin which is in my members. (Romans 7:23)

The collective may not be in Captivity whereas certain individuals may be. Sin is the way in. Any sin.

Jonah's captivity was uniquely described in the Bible, but it assuredly was captivity. The whole world lies in darkness--, the belly of a whale? We may surmise that hell is vast, the devil has a whale of a prison because too many people are there.

1. **Lord, help. Lord, deliver us today, from every captivity, in the Name of Jesus.**

Job was certainly held captive in the spirit, and we know this because of all that happened to him in the natural. No one can go through that level of loss, torment, destruction, hurt and pain unless they are in Captivity.

We are so against corporeal punishment in the natural, but shall we say nothing about it in the spirit?

What?

We cry out against bullying in the natural, but in the spirit, does the devil get to do as he chooses? No, we must do something about it. If we see something, we say something – we pray something.

We are definitely against child abuse and spousal abuse in the natural, but are we praying for our children and one another, that others can be released from Captivity when all manner of things could be happening to them? In Captivity, it is as though the devil's program is: *Hold still, while I take stuff from you and do stuff to you. Stay here and take it.*

This is why I said at the beginning of this book that Captivity is the problem. The sun, in and of itself won't do things to us, the moon, the stars, the planets, the elements were all created to give Glory to God. If they give glory to God, then they are not for the hurt or harm of His creation or mankind, whom He loves so much.

Captivity allows whomever or whatever wants to do harm to God's creation, to do that harm. God's creation has to be reprogrammed against man, although temporarily, be it the elements or humans, to the elements or to the humans. Or to the elements against the humans. This is why we command the day and also the night, it is to reprogram back to factory settings the program that God has in His Creation and negate and nullify the evil programming in the elements by evil human agents. Evil programming is for hurt, harm, and the captivity of other humans. People were not created or designed to do harm to others; it is the devil that they worship, the devil gets in them and makes them do things unholy and out of God's plans for mankind.

For, lo, the wicked bend their bow, they make ready their arrow upon the string, that they may privily shoot at the upright in heart. (Psalm 11:2)

No, saints of God. NO! God, forbid. Well, God did forbid. Although the wages of sin is death, God has not given us over to death, but we are paying for iniquity.

2.   Lord, return our Captivity, in the Name of Jesus.

3.   Lord, forgive our sins and iniquity and bring us out of captivity, in the Name of Jesus.

4.   Lord, even though my spouse hurt me, I realize that they may be in Captivity and must do the things they do. Lord, forgive my spouse for their sins against You, blot out their iniquity and return their Captivity, so that they can return wholly and whole to You, and also to our marriage, in the Name of Jesus.

5. Lord, even though my child is getting on my last nerve, it is not about me right now. Whatever my child has done please forgive them. Whatever I have done, or even my child's other parent is waving a flag of iniquity to the Captivity *spirit*, forgive us and wash away all iniquity on both sides of my child's bloodline. Lord, rescue my child from Captivity and let them return to me, to us, to our family, to their normal self, or even better, in the Name of Jesus.

And the LORD turned the captivity of Job, when he prayed for his friends: also the LORD gave Job twice as much as he had before. (Job 42:10)

Paul & Silas may or may not have remembered what was recorded in the Old Testament when they were locked up, in a physical prison in the natural realm. Were Paul and Silas locked up in spiritual prison or a natural prison? Or were they locked up in *both*?

At any rate, they had either learned how to get out, or they were so filled with the Spirit of God and had such faith in God that they simply praised Him anyway. Job said, *Though he slay me, yet will I trust in him* (Job 13:15A).

The following is based on an excerpt from my book, **Let Them Come Up & Worship**:

"We learned in Exodus that God will let even a slave go when certain conditions are met. A slave is the ultimate captive. If there is a purpose in your being set free, if you are coming up to worship the Lord God, then God will come Himself, or send someone, spiritually and or naturally to get you out of captivity. As long as you are alive, as long as there is life, there is hope. Even if you are in captivity, as long as you are alive you can get out. After death, that is another whole story which you will not like. Even if you think your idols are helping you and giving you the good life on this side, Hell is another whole story, and it is eternal."

Your Authority

Bringing into *captivity* every thought to the
obedience of Christ. (2 Corinthians 10:5)

Most of us well know that when we hear a
word from a prophet and we don't like it, we
sometimes resent the speaker. Even if God told that
person to say that, and to say it that certain way. Jesus
decried Jerusalem for killing the prophets. This had to
be said since the prophets speak what *thus saith the
Lord,* and then and even now can be very unpopular.

When a demon, devil, or idol comes to you
with a crooked thought, we don't ponder it over and
figure out how to do that mischievous, devilish, evil
thing, we cast it down, we cast it out. We must
recognize what is an evil prophecy. We compare that
word to the Word of God, and we bring it into the
obedience of Christ. As faith comes by hearing, then
this evil entity which brought you a wicked thought
may be considered an evil prophet – that's a prophet
you should kill, not the prophets of God.

I see another law in my members--bringing me
into *captivity* to the law of sin. (Romans 7:23)

People of the Captivity

And go, get thee to them of the captivity, unto the children of thy people, and speak unto them, and tell them, Thus saith the Lord GOD; whether they will hear, or whether they will forbear. (Ezekiel 3:11)

When you begin to be addressed collectively as *people of the Captivity* – you've got a real problem.

It is difficult to impossible to hear the Word of God while in Captivity. Maybe it is out of range of the Holy Spirit? Maybe the Holy Spirit's signals are blocked? Maybe the din of the place of Captivity is so loud and confusing that the captive doesn't know what he's hearing or what to actually believe. It could be all of that, and so much more, such as the evil anointing on the lies and propaganda being spoken to itching ears, and silly people. So, God sends His Word and says, **Tell them, whether they listen or not. Whether they heed or not, tell them.** That's also Mercy, saints of God because God didn't give up on us, even in captivity. And, a Word from God is like good news from home. The Word of God has power to perform. The Word of God can set us free: He sent His Word and healed them. Being healed from Captivity is being set free. A Word from God is something you can stand on; use it to lift you up even if you have to climb out of a window of that prison to escape and be free.

Afterwards the spirit took me up, and brought me in a vision by the Spirit of God into Chaldea, to them of the captivity. So the vision that I had seen went up from me.

Then I spake unto them of the captivity all the things that the LORD had shewed me.
(Ezekiel 11:24-25)

Then shalt thou bring forth thy stuff by day in their sight, as stuff for removing: and thou shalt go forth at even in their sight, as they that go forth into captivity.

And I did so as I was commanded: I brought forth my stuff by day, as stuff for captivity, and in the even I digged through the wall with mine hand; I brought *it* forth in the twilight, *and* I bare *it* upon *my* shoulder in their sight.
(Ezekiel 12:4,7)

Say, I *am* your sign: like as I have done, so shall it be done unto them: they shall remove *and* go into captivity. (Ezekiel 12:11)

When God tells a people they are going into captivity, He means it. He got the prophet to demonstrate how to do it, like lining up on a cruise ship before it sets sail to learn your muster station.

And it came to pass in the twelfth year of our captivity, in the tenth *month*, in the fifth *day* of the month, *that* one that had escaped out of

Jerusalem came unto me, saying, The city is smitten.
(Ezekiel 33:21)

And the heathen shall know that the house of
Israel went into captivity for their iniquity: because
they trespassed against me, therefore hid I my
face from them, and gave them into the hand of
their enemies: so fell they all by the sword.
(Ezekiel 39:23)

This is part of the drudgery of Captivity. The captives began to count time by the length of their captivity, like placing marks on the wall of the jail cell. Only thing, they were marking years and not days, weeks, or months. The captive Jews were staring down an evil timeline, a satanic timeline.

In the five and twentieth year of our captivity, in the
beginning of the year, in the tenth *day* of the
month, in the fourteenth year after that the city was
smitten, in the selfsame day the hand of the
LORD was upon me, and brought me thither.
(Ezekiel 40:1)

And they that understand among the people shall
instruct many: yet they shall fall by the sword, and
by flame, by captivity, and by spoil, *many* days.
(Daniel 11:33)

Who wants to be known by what they've been through? No one, unless you have an overcoming testimony. But you still do not want to be called the thing you used to be. Not only that, you do not want to have been in a situation or a bad condition for so long that you now have been named that affliction. No one wants to be nicknamed the thing that was most embarrassing, humiliating, or painful and for that nickname to stick.

Years before I was ever a thought in my daddy's mind, seems he hurt his foot, or toe while either playing or working outside. His brothers nicknamed him, Hop and yes, it stuck. All of his life he answered to that. For the average person, it would bring back that memory, but my dad was okay with it. Still, perhaps he shouldn't have been. Evil names can even be nicknames with no evil intent behind them, but every time a particular name is called, it could bind or limit a person.

A person could be in Captivity to a name or by a name. There are so many ways of Captivity. When the devil gets your friends and family involved in your captivity, he's pretty much got you surrounded.

> Then was Daniel brought in before the king. *And* the king spake and said unto Daniel, *Art* thou that Daniel, which *art* of the children of the captivity of Judah, whom the king my father brought out of Jewry? (Daniel 5:13)

> Then answered they and said before the king, That Daniel, which *is* of the children of the captivity of Judah, regardeth not thee, O king, nor the decree that (Daniel 6:13)

Well, you can't misunderstand it—if someone will tell you over and again that you are a captive, or you are *of the Captivity*. But it is limiting. It is disenfranchising, it is diminishing it continually puts one in their place. It can be condemning, dehumanizing, and it can make a person feel either outraged or belittled. Captivity is not a club that anyone should seek. There is no prestige in it; it says you are a slave, you are property and that you are nothing.

Captivity is a gated community that you DO NOT want to be in.

In Christ, none of that is true for you, however. So to get out of spiritual Captivity, no matter where your body is, you've got to change how you think. You have to change what is on your mind. You've got to think on *these things*, (Philippians 4:8) as well as study all of the Word of God.

The Whole World Lies in Darkness

The whole world lies in darkness.

And we know that we are of God, and the whole world lieth in wickedness. (1 John 5:19)

We know that we are from God, and the whole world lies in the power of the evil one. (1 John 5:19. ESV)

Satan rules as a tyrant who has "weakened the nations" (Isa 14:12), and currently "deceives the whole world" (Rev 12:9).

Satan appears to be the father of fascism. Fascism is authoritarian, and ultranationalist ideology, characterized by a dictatorial leader, centralized autocracy, militarism, forcible suppression of opposition. The devil is merciless and wants absolute control over you, and everything you have or ever will have. Unfortunately, Satan is the prince of this world so if Jesus Christ is not chosen as your Lord and Savior, you automatically serve the autocrat, the devil.

The devil is not a joke, nor is he powerless. If you do not rise up in the position and authority given to you by being in Christ Jesus, you will simply be a pawn to be used and pushed around even all your life by the devil. You may not even realize that is happening to you, if you are not paying attention and believe in a *that's just the way life is* philosophy.

Darkness is default for his Earth, you have to ask for the Light. Many times, you may have to demand that the darkness leave, especially if you purposefully, or even accidentally invited it into your life. Especially if your ancestors left you this gift of sinful darkness and never fought the battle to remove it before you were born, tag---, *you're it*. Fight it, or pass it on to your children and their children. Sin inhabits the darkness. Once captive, the devil endeavors to keep his captive in the dark, unaware, ignorant, without knowledge, Wisdom, or understanding.

Saints of God, we are called children of Light.

Ye are all the children of light, and the children of the day: we are not of the night, nor of darkness.

Therefore let us not sleep, as do others; but let us watch and be sober.

For they that sleep sleep in the night; and they that be drunken are drunken in the night.

But let us, who are of the day, be sober, putting on the breastplate of faith and love; and for an helmet, the hope of salvation. (1 Thessalonians 5:5-8)

Gnashing of Teeth

But the children **of** the kingdom shall be cast
out into outer darkness: there shall
be weeping and **gnashing of teeth.** (Matthew 8:12)

I am a dentist, and I see A LOT of bruxism in my dental practice. In dental terms it is clenching or grinding of the teeth. Biblically, it denotes extreme anguish and utter despair of men consigned to eternal punishment in hell. Have you ever seen an actor flex the muscles of his face? That is one of the primary muscles used in this gnashing. When this muscle and others go into spasm, man, oh man does it hurt. For this reason, I do not recommend that anyone practice building up this muscle in that way.

Anyhow, it also denotes snarling and growling: in the sense of biting. A bruxer can put 900 lbs. of pressure per square inch on their teeth. This is a recipe for destruction of dentition and also the jawbone, over time.

This is mentioned because I query all my bruxers and they are having horrific dreams at night, which is when most of this bruxism and gnashing is going on. Folks, these people are captive, and they are working, working, working, trying to get out of captivity every night. Do they get out? Many get close or almost out but then they remain in Captivity. Gritting your teeth together won't solve a spiritual problem. You need to work while it is day to get out of Captivity. You need to ask the Lord to give you spiritual awareness in the dream so you can walk, talk, and speak with authority within the dream and speak to Captivity and demand by the power in the Blood of Jesus to be set free. Or, you may ask the Lord to send forth mighty Angels to bind Captivity – since Jesus already did that, and set you free.

In the daytime do any and all of these in any and every combination: pray, read your Bible—especially out loud, fast, seek deliverance, praise and worship, and make sacrificial offerings to the Lord.

But the children of the kingdom shall be cast
out into outer darkness: there shall
be weeping and gnashing of teeth. (Matthew 8:12)

The gnashing of teeth is a symptom and a sign to you that something is wrong. You may not know exactly what it is, but you are struggling because you are in Captivity and trying to get out.

And shall cast them into a furnace of fire: there shall
be wailing and **gnashing of teeth**. (Matthew 13:42)[h]

There shall be weeping and gnashing of teeth, when
ye shall see Abraham, and Isaac, and Jacob, and all
the prophets, in the kingdom of God, and you
yourselves thrust out. (Luke 13:28)

The bitter end to the disobedience of God.

How To Know If You are Captive

Parts of this chapter are excerpted from my book, **Souls in Captivity**.

When a soul is captured spiritually, there is often no natural evidence of the captivity unless a discerning person knows what to look for. Sometimes the person cannot see himself as captured because he *is* captured. Don't kidnappers put blindfolds or head coverings on their victims? This is where one-another ministry comes in. This is where the five-fold ministry gifts come in. Someone will tell you if things aren't quite right with you.

Will you listen? Will you hear? *Can you?*

Foremost, the sign that a person is captured is frustration, delays, and restrictions. He can't seem to get ahead, try as he may. He may not be trying anymore, because he may have already given up.

Too many men are running away from great women to avoid marriage because they don't want to be "trapped," not realizing that the reason they have blocked marriage and God's will out of their plans and out of their lives is because a part of their heart is already captured by evil; it is not available for real love. No woman will ever be able to "trap" him because the devil already has these men "trapped," captive. They will not fulfill God's will for their lives in marriage and having righteous seed (children).

Here are some signs that your soul is captive in case you are wondering if you are.

The Devil Loves Trauma. A major trauma or disappointment, loss, broken heart—anything that has traumatized you significantly even to distraction is an open door for the devil to fragment or capture your soul. Have you sustained at least one major trauma in your life? That trauma had a purpose. And, then he will do it again and again to take more and more of your soul, especially if you don't heal from the first time.

A major trauma can hinder a person for a long time, especially if we stay there in that trauma. And, especially-especially if we rehearse it either over and again in our minds, or verbally to anyone who will listen.

Once a *spirit of captivity* has taken root in your life, your life can change dramatically, drastically. This person can end up with a victim mentality, always expecting the worst. They can seclude themselves and become lonely, adopting a *what's the use* attitude. Apathy may follow, then they may go into a depression and that is a way the devil can get more of their soul.

Yes, there is Salvation--, thank You, Jesus, and there is Deliverance.

A *spirit of captivity* will destroy purpose and destiny. After deliverance, the demons may be gone, but have they left a mark or an imprint on you? If captivity has affected you, you will behave differently than before, while not even realizing it. (Romans 12:1-2)

Apostle Paul pleads with us to keep our flesh under submission of the Spirit of God. Don't sin. With all that is in you, don't sin, by help of the Holy Spirit. Let our minds be transformed and become more like Christ, being remade into His likeness day by day.

Symptoms of Captivity: Sickness, disease, poverty; this is the Curse of the Law. Fear, frustration, loneliness, nothing is working. Loss at the verge of success. Tormenting dreams. Can't sleep—more torment. Gnashing of teeth. *Monitoring spirits*—you sense, see or feel their presence.

Being fed in the dream; you are captive. Being defiled in the dream; that is not free sex, that is defilement; you are captive. When a person is captive the captor can do anything they want to them, and at any time. Sleep paralysis. Strange people in the dream. Spirit spouse. Feeling robotic; just going through the motions in waking life. Doing things that are out of character, and then wondering why you did those things. Dreams of being guarded. Dreams of policemen that are not helping you. Dreams of being lost in a forest, especially a dark forest.

The worst: when a person "blacks out" and later wakes up in a place, doing a thing, and they don't even know how they got there, or what they did. That's full possession; full captivity.

The Spirit of the Lord God is upon me because the Lord has anointed me to bring good news to the afflicted; He has sent me to bind up the brokenhearted, to proclaim liberty to the captives, and freedom to prisoners. (Isaiah 61:1)

Why all this talk in the Bible of Captivity and prisons and prisoners unless there is something to it?

To open blind eyes, To bring prisoners from the dungeon and those who dwell in darkness from the prison. (Isaiah 42:7)

To hear the groaning of the prisoner, to set free those who were doomed to death, (Psalm 102:20)

The captive is often bowed down, pressed down, lying down in sin, in his own polluted blood.

For innumerable evils have compassed me about: mine iniquities have taken hold upon me, so that I am not able to look up; they are more than the hairs of mine head: therefore my heart faileth me. (Psalm 40:12)

Separate body parts can get captured. Whatever you sinned with is a very likely candidate for capturing. Perhaps this is why Jesus said, if your eye offend you, pluck it out. If your hand offends you, cut it off.

How does your head get captured? What did your head do? Did it think on wrong thoughts? Did it look on wrong things, listen to wrong things? Perhaps any and all of that. Perhaps more than that. The head may be spiritually captured; we are not talking about heads in a duffle bag. Ways a head may be captured.

- Evil dreams.
- Trigger dreams. You must remember all dreams and cancel demonic dreams and any intended initiation, dedication, or planned evil outcome because of those dreams, in the Name of Jesus.
- Evil summons.
- Evil handshake.
- Evil laying on of hands.
- Evil touch.
- Evil exchange.
- Masquerade.
- Evil veil.
- Covering cast.
- Incision (tattoos are so dangerous), but there are spiritual tattoos some you cannot even see.
- Evil marks.
- Sleeping with demonic, wicked, occultic, humans or others – every person is not necessarily a person.

- Evil barber/backbiting, evil hairdresser.
- Demonic hair products.
- Trauma/traumatic brain injury- you may have fallen or gotten clocked in the head.
- Soul ties.
- Spirit marriages.

6. Lord, locate me, by the power in the Blood of Jesus. Locate my head, in the Name of Jesus.

7. My destiny, be unlocked and uncaged, in the Name of Jesus.

8. Household and *familiar spirit* witchcraft, fail against me, in the Name of Jesus.

9. Lord, if I come from a bloodline of captured minds, souls, or heads, I repent for myself and my ancestors. Lord, forgive all sin, remove iniquity and remove this curse from my family bloodline, in the Name of Jesus.

10. If my spouse comes from a foundation of captivity, especially of the head, LORD, remove this curse from their foundation that our family may live and thrive, in the Name of Jesus.

11. I bind the work of every backbiting evil hairdresser and barber against me, and my spouse and family, in the Name of Jesus.

12. Holy Spirit, show me demonic haircare products, processes, and styles, so that I may remove and destroy them today, in the Name of Jesus.

13. Evil touch on my head; I break your power by the Power in the Blood of Jesus.

14. Backbiting, evil pronouncements upon my life, lose your power over me; I break your curse, in the Name of Jesus.

15. All my glory stolen from me from birth until now, I command you to return to me, in the Name of Jesus; Lord deal with the thief or thieves involved in taking my glory, in the Name of Jesus.

16. Evil mark and every mark of failure, blood of Jesus, blot it off me and out of my life, in the Name of Jesus.

17. My crown of good success, return to me now, in the Name of Jesus.

18. Covering cast, evil veil, masquerade hiding my head, catch fire and be removed from my head forever, in the Name of Jesus.

19. Lord, let my destiny helpers and all divine connections find me now, in the Name of Jesus.

20. Demonic cages hiding my true identity, blocking my helpers from reaching me, I command you to break completely, in Jesus' Name.

21. Evil summons, I will not answer you, I will not obey your evil instructions, by the power in the Blood of Jesus.

22. Any demonic hand touching me, pressing my head down, saying I shall not rise, you are a liar; I shall rise—you fall down and die, in the Name of Jesus.

23. All rejection in my life turn to favor and celebration now, in the Name of Jesus.

24. I receive full deliverance from my head, by Fire in Jesus' Name. (adapted from the book: **Anatomy of Deliverance** by Olyumi Stephen Beloved)

Symptoms of Captivity

If the enemy captures your head, he has captured 7 of the 9 gates of your body. Gates are places of power and authority; they control what goes in and what comes out. You can starve a city by causing a famine; you can send in invaders; you can send in lies and all manner of evil by controlling a gate of a nation. It is a powerful blessing to be able to do so. It is a curse when your enemies control your gates.

> Your descendants will conquer the cities of their enemies. (Genesis 22:17)

In your *feels, when* the mind is captured: a person may feel depressed, forgetful, hurt,

- Prayer life has dried up.
- Mind wandering.
- Sleep wave.
- Severe unexplainable headaches.
- Blank mind.
- Brain fog.
- Accident prone. Mishaps and missteps – for all you know you are tripped up in the spirit, and then it manifests in the natural to let you know

that something is wrong. Most of us check ourselves physically after this happens, and many times we need to. But, do we ever check ourselves spiritually to see why this happened?

- Forgetfulness.—senior moments – I've told you that senior moments is not to be laughed at or accepted – it is demonic.
- Confusion/ lack of concentration, especially when reading the Bible.
- Feeling things crawling or moving in your head (have you been eating in the dream in the past and haven't dealt with it?)
- Dream afflictions—crazy dreams and nightmares almost every night.
- Evil visions as soon as you close your eyes.
- Feeling controlled.
- Seeing dead people in your dreams/hallucinations in the daytime.
- Thoughts of the dead, thoughts of death or suicide. Those are not your thoughts! that is demonic. that is demons on assignment trying to drive you nuts, yes, but also trying to get you to agree with their death program for your life, or do nothing about what they are sending to you so by doing nothing you agree with them.

25. I cast down every evil imagination that exalts itself against the knowledge of God, in the Name of Jesus.

26. Every thought, image and word of death, I bind you and cast you out of my mind and out of my heart, now in the Name of Jesus. GO! Go! Go! You must go, in the Name of Jesus.

27. Every thought, image, or word of suicide or hopelessness, I bind you and cast you and every demon promoting such an attack against me, OUT, OUT, OUT, in the Name of Jesus.

28. Every curse of personal destruction or suicide sent to me from any origin at any time, from any entity or evil human agent, lose your power, and leave my life NOW, in the Name of Jesus.

29. I vomit out all spiritual food and beverage eaten in the dream, in the Name of Jesus.

30. I reverse all damage done to me because of evil spirit food, in the Name of Jesus.

31. Night caterers of evil spiritual food fed to me, forced on me, or given to me in the dream, I reject all food and beverage, I reject you, EAT your own food, drink your own beverage and fall down and die, in the Name of Jesus.

32. Anything implanted or moving in my body, my head, or anywhere in my body because of evil spiritual food, come out, come out, come out now, with all your roots, and have no effect on me, by the power in the Blood of Jesus.

33. I shall live. I shall live. I shall live. I shall live and not die, and declare the goodness of the lord, in the Name of Jesus.

34. I shall live until I am satisfied, and in divine health, Godly health, perfect health, vitality, vigor and in prosperity, in the Name of Jesus.

35. Every masquerade keeping me in grief, excessive grief, or pulling me down to the grave, by the power in the Blood of Jesus I command you to leave my dreams, my life, my mind and my consciousness, in the Name of Jesus.

36. My deceased loved ones are in the arms of the LORD, they are not with me, visiting me, or talking to me. According to the Word of God, the dead know nothing, therefore I have no need to ask or tell them anything in the Name of Jesus.

37. I will not be drawn to the grave, or be a victim of untimely death, especially not by demons

masquerading as dead celebrities, friends or relatives, in the Name of Jesus.

38. I shall live until I am satisfied, and in divine health, Godly health, perfect health, vitality, vigor and in prosperity, in the Name of Jesus.

Acute or chronic anger is one of the most common signs of captivity. Add to that, arrogance and pride. *Pride comes before the fall.*

For thought: ADAM & EVE took food from the Serpent who fell from Heaven, like lightning because of PRIDE. What happened to Adam & Eve next? They FELL from their God created positions and lost their home, their PARADISE.

Reject spirit food, no matter what it is called – an apple? Reject food from the prideful – PRIDE COMES BEFORE the FALL.

Pride goeth before destruction, and an haughty spirit before a fall. (Proverbs 16:18).

FYI: Pride is acquired rather recently, whereas haughtiness is a type of pride that a person is born with. It is often found in the silver spoon crowd and the privileged. There is another form of pride in the wicked. Occultic bloodlines are prideful because they feel they have powers and secrets that others do not have or know about.

People do the bidding of whose table they sit at if there is a demonic anointing on that table. The prophets that ate at Jezebel's table did her bidding. Have you noticed how many meals are in mafia movies? Eating together, or eating food that has been dedicated with or without your knowledge seals deals and covenants.

In the spirit and dream do not eat; spirits don't need food. In the natural, do not eat at everyone's table. Use discernment or risk being captured by food – natural or *spirit* food.

Physical Signs of Captivity

When the enemy of our souls wants to capture a person, many times the first thing they try to capture is the head. Eventually head or mind Captivity may show up in the **physical**. In the New Testament, there was a man by the pool of Bethesda who said he had no one to put him in. That man was lame, and we think that is a very serious issue; and it is. Moreover, it is a physical manifestation of a very serious **spiritual** issue.

There was a woman, elsewhere in the NT who was bowed over for many years, that was another, but different manifestation of a spiritual affliction. Jesus delivered them both. Jesus delivered them spiritually. When He did, the Word often says, *and immediately.* Jesus wasn't doing spinal surgery in the natural, if He had, immediately the lame man and the bowed over woman would have done nothing but lay there in Recovery, then go through Rehab or PT, and after many days or weeks, their situations would have been corrected.

Jesus is our Deliverer, spiritually and then the spiritual changes manifest immediately in the natural.

Doctors and surgeons and other professionals do things for others in the natural; but unless their patients are changed spiritually by the Spirit of God, then they are still the same and still could be captive, even while the manifestation of captivity is no longer evident, or as evident in the natural.

For example, a woman sneezes and sneezes in her home. She is allergic to dust and dust mites. Instead of removing the dust, she goes to the pharmacy and gets an allergy medication. She takes one or two of those pills daily and lives with her dust, which may not even be visible, but it is there. Spiritual issues may not be evident in the natural or barely noticeable, like *dust*.

A man has orthopedic surgery because of severe, bone on bone joint pain. He now feels better and walks better after some months. Was the spiritual cause of that orthopedic problem ever addressed? Or, was it just masked by taking away the *symptoms* that man could feel, or didn't like? Even in medical school we are taught that most people don't want to stop certain behaviors, they just want a pill to make them feel better so they can continue to do as they have always done.

A spiritual change takes choice and will power and the Spirit of God. After a spiritual change, immediately there can be a natural healing, but after a natural surgery or "healing", there may not be a spiritual change at all. So, will the person relapse back into the same issue? Or, will the person begin to manifest another issue to replace the one that was just "fixed"? Only God knows.

Therefore, pray for deliverance before, as, and after you get pain relieved, maladies, and symptoms corrected in the natural, by any means you may get things corrected, *medically,* but that doesn't change the spiritual makeup of things, and the spiritual is the source of the adverse natural manifestation.

They say free your mind and the rest will follow. Your mind is part of your soul, so that makes sense, but also free your spirit and the manifestations of freedom will gloriously show up in your life, the natural realm, to glorify God, and sometimes immediately. I am not saying to shun medical treatment; many times, that is your deliverance, as the leaves on the trees are for the healing of the nations. Be sure you get your spiritual deliverance as well as natural, since natural solutions do not fix spiritual problems.

Another example is crooked teeth. You may wear and now have worn braces and now have the straightest teeth, but when you have children--, they may have your crooked teeth because crooked teeth are in your family's spiritual foundation.

Physical signs of captivity include:

- Worry and anxiety
- Excessive worry,
- Tension, irritation.
- Problems appear HUGE and they may not be.
- On edge.
- Restlessness
- Muscle tension and aches.
- Headaches of any kind. For all you know, you may have just been knocked upside the head in the spirit by a jailor or your captor and then it manifests in the natural.
- Any pain, sudden, acute, or chronic and repetitive, in one particular place or that moves around.
- Confusion. I include mental conditions such as over-grieving, hoarding, and uncleanliness in this category.
- Sweating.
- Nausea/ indigestion.
- New and sudden allergies.
- Frequent bathroom breaks.
- Fidgeting—no Peace.
- Can't sleep. Can't fall asleep. Can't stay asleep.
- Exhaustion/tiredness.

I cried unto the Lord with my voice, and he heard me out of his holy hill. Selah.

I laid me down and slept; I awaked; for
the Lord sustained me.

I will not be afraid of ten thousands of people,
that have set themselves against me round about.

Arise, O Lord; save me, O my God: for thou hast
smitten all mine enemies upon the cheek bone;
thou hast broken the teeth of the ungodly.

Salvation belongeth unto the Lord: thy blessing
is upon thy people. Selah. (Psalm 3: 4-8)

- Tremors, trembling
- Easily startled/unsettled.
- Numb hands and feet
- Difficulty swallowing
- Breathing difficulty, (sporadically)
- Twitching
- Hot flashes
- Hives/rashes
- Cravings
- Urges
- Poor decisions
- Unforced errors.

Many of these are signs of witchcraft attack as well, which I go over at length in my book: **Upgrade: How to Get Out of Survival Mode**. Read free on Kindle; many of my books are free to read on Kindle.

Other Body Parts

Besides the head, other body parts can be captured and tortured or abused in spiritual realms. One part is the leg. This manifests in certain ways if a person's leg or legs are captured.

> And he that was dead came forth, bound hand and foot with graveclothes: and his face was bound about with a napkin. Jesus saith unto them, Loose him, and let him go. (John 11:44)

Lazarus was bound hand and foot with graveclothes; most often we think of this as what was done after he died. Well, yes, in the natural, but was he bound hand and foot in the spirit **before** he died? Perhaps by an evil jailer in Captivity?

> Then said the king to the servants, Bind him hand and foot, and take him away, and cast *him* into outer darkness; there shall be weeping and gnashing of teeth. (Matthew 22:13)

- The captured leg may be in pain when no other body part is, and there is no medical reason for this pain.
- Pain in the leg may be called sciatica or nerve damage in the natural. Sure, go to your doctor, but pray for deliverance of the leg from witchcraft covens first, in the Name of Jesus.
- The captured leg makes a person late everywhere they go. Man, whole people groups may have captured legs.
- The captured leg makes a person try and try but not be successful in their business and other endeavors.
- A captured leg affects your prosperity and limits one to poverty.
- Repeated failures, pray for deliverance of the leg.
- If you are captured or defeated in a dream, pray immediately for deliverance of the leg.
- Your leg may feel like it has been stabbed or an arrow shot through it, very suddenly.

    39. Witchcraft arrow fired into my leg, come out and return to sender, in the Name of Jesus.

    40. My leg, be delivered from every witchcraft coven or satanic altar, in the Name of Jesus.

41. Every obstacle, bondage, delay or stagnation planned or established against my life, break, break, in the Name of Jesus.

42. I dismantle every curse spoken against my legs and my deliverance, in the Name of Jesus.

43. Marine kingdom embargoes set against my legs, come out and roast to ashes by Fire, in the Name of Jesus.

44. Arrows of laziness and procrastination fired at me, I fire you back, seven-fold, in the Name of Jesus.

45. Arrows of backwardness or failure fired against my legs, come out with all your roots and have no effect against my destiny and success, in the Name of Jesus.

46. Every evil arrow fired against my legs to make me walk away from my marriage or relationships, I pull you out by Fire. Return to sender, in Jesus' Name.

47. Lord, help me – I command every negative spiritual projection into my mind, soul, and life to be uprooted and burned to ashes, now, in the Name of Jesus.

48. Every witchcraft attack—back to sender, in the Name of Jesus.

49. *Spirits of confusion* and *uncertainty*, you are bound by the power in the Name of Jesus and cast out of my life forever.

50. Lord, restore and repair all damage done to my spirit, soul, and body by demonic attacks that have come against my head and mind, in the Name of Jesus.

51. I bind and cast out the *spirit of fear* for the LORD has not given me the *spirit of fear*, but one of LOVE, power, and a sound mind, in the Name of Jesus, Amen.

52. Every evil and demonic imagination in the heart of evil human persecutors who have arisen against me and my family, I cast them down and bring them to nothing by the power in the Blood of Jesus.

53. My body, soul and spirit, resist the evil imaginations of self and of others, in the Name of Jesus.

54. Lord, cleanse my head from every evil thought, in the Name of Jesus.

55. Let the words of my mouth and the meditation of my heart be acceptable to you, my Lord, my strength and my Redeemer, in Jesus' Name.

How Might One Be Captive?

Witchcrafts and the occult have devised all kinds of ways that a person or some body part may be rendered captive. I will list some of the containers that the spiritual representation of a person is locked away in. How it is done is not anything I would want to ever teach anyone. Just know that it is done.

- Pots
- Jars
- Ropes
- Chains
- Irons
- Fetters
- Bars
- Padlocks
- Cages
- Prison
- Jail
- Grave/burial
- Any element
- Any celestial body
- Imprisoned Mentally
- Imprisoned Emotionally

- Imprisoned and bound by sickness, disease, disorder, illness, syndromes and symptoms.
- Imprisoned spiritually, trapped in vanity, pride, etc. grief, broken heart, depression, anger, rage

All of you may be captured, or just one part or two. Parts of you could be in different places of Captivity, even at the same time. This is why we pray:

56. Lord, search the land of the living and the dead, and locate me; gather me back together, in the Name of Jesus.

A person you dated and didn't even know they were a witch could have your manhood or your womb in a jar or a pot. Another witch could be jealous of your financial success and may have caged your leg. Another evil network may be specialists at padlocking or imprisoning in some other way. I talk about flesh hell, soul hell, and spirit hell in my book, **WTH? Get Me Out of This HELL.**

Folks, there could be multiple altars fighting against you. There is no time to sit around. You need to be in prayer and also practicing the disciplines of your faith.

Pray against these modalities if prompted by the Holy Spirit, pray to be released from any and all of these holding methods. Each one could be a whole book unto itself, so we will not detail them here. They are listed for your information and direction.

If one or more causes a reaction when you read them, find a deliverance minister or at least locate one online and get your freedom.

It may be best to break free of one modality at a time. Prayers with fasting is always more effective.

Your Real Life

We've all seen enough prison movies to know what happens in a prison. Is any of that stuff happening to you in your dream life? Your dream life is your spiritual life and that is your real life. What is happening there is what is really happening to you, and if it doesn't stop happening eventually it may happen in the natural. Even if it never happens in the natural, you do not want what is happening to you in the spirit, if it is foul, bad, evil, not of God to keep happening. Nor do you want it to be your case permanently.

While there is life, there is hope. You must get yourself out of captivity. You are not left alone; the Lord will never leave or forsake you, but, you have to let your intentions be known to the Lord in prayers, supplications, offerings, sacrifices, dedication, devotion, fasting, decrees, and declarations. You must take out the weapons of your warfare and begin to do battle against your Captor to turn your captivity around. The Lord will join you. If He wee simply going to get you out with no effort on your part, you wouldn't even be in there in the first place.

You're Being *Fed*?

Oh, you don't believe you are in captivity? Read on.

In the natural, if something is going on with your stomach or your gut, you are in captivity. That is one of the first things they mess with. Any abnormality at all – trace it back to the first day you remember a problem – you have most likely been captured. I can tell you, with my cast iron stomach, that I had bragged about for decades, saying, *Oh, I can eat anything*, one day that changed.

Well folks, I was on holiday on a certain island, in a Hispanic country. I ate some food that said, *No way we are staying in there*, and up it came – all night. That was many years ago. I can blame it on the food. I can blame it on Montezuma, whom I do not worship. I can blame it on food poisoning, or on chance. No, it was witchcraft.

My stomach and digestive tract have finally been sorted out, because I've been fully delivered from witchcraft. By looking back at the timing and the symptoms I can tell you who did this. Man, they must be suffering now for messing with a Child of God who sends witchcraft arrows back to sender.

Saints of God, do not gain any faith for anything **negative** I say, the unsavory things that I must write are written for instruction only. Put your faith in what the Word says and what God says, only. In the natural they say that gut problems are the beginning of the dying process. That does not have to be so because you can be delivered mightily by the Spirit of God.

On deliverance ground you hear many deliverance ministers say that many demons live in the gut. All of that could be true, so these demons get in there and mess up the balance of things that God has established as good health. They make you crave things you don't normally eat. They make you push away things that are good for you that you normally do eat. They want you to take on their nature. They want you to eat what they want. They are *spirits*, none of that stuff can hurt them, but what they want you to eat is usually destructive to you. And, no matter which direction, whether you'll blow up like a blowfish, or shrink down to skin and bones--, it will be to extremes, excess, and to your demise.

They want to feed you. In the natural they want to choose the destructive foods you will intake. In the spirit they want to feed you spirit food in the dream so they control, control, and control you, both now and later. Spirit food initiates you into witchcraft, but it can also lie dormant like a time bomb until the devil decides to detonate it. And, you. Many times, the ingesting of *spirit food* is the origin of diseases and illness in a person.

A deliverance minister, Apostle Chipoyera says that the Holy Spirit told him that there are no fat, old men; lose weight. Lose weight and live. Ideally, losing weight purges that gut and if that weight loss is a fast that is dedicated to the Lord it will cleanse you of evil that should not have residence in your gut.

> *Is* this not the fast that I have chosen:
> To loose the bonds of wickedness,
> To undo the heavy burdens,
> To let the oppressed go free,
> And that you break every yoke?
> *Is it* not to share your bread with the hungry,
> And that you bring to your house the poor who
> are cast out;
> When you see the naked, that you cover him,
> And not hide yourself from your own flesh?
> Then your light shall break forth like the morning,
> Your healing shall spring forth speedily,
> And your righteousness shall go before you;
> The glory of the Lord shall be your rear guard.
> Then you shall call, and the Lord will answer;
> You shall cry, and He will say, 'Here I *am.*'
> (Isaiah 58:6-9)

Saints of God, before I was moved to begin writing this book, I upped my prayer time because I wanted to, not for any physical reasons. I upped it because if I was bound in any captivity at all, I wanted to pray my way out of it. As soon as I added an extra 2 hours to my usual prayer watch (over the day, not necessarily all at once) people started commenting that I had lost weight.

I was still eating pretty much the same foods as always. Anyway, I realized immediately that I had lost INFLAMMATION. That is deliverance, and now I'm easily dropping weight that so easily beset me, when I was trying very hard not to be beset by weight.

That excess weight that we call obesity is not obesity**; that is the need for deliverance**. Exercise, diet, take weight loss meds, have surgery – do what you like, as approved by God, but do the spiritual work first. We are vessels designed to carry the glory of God. We are the temple of the Holy Spirit, but when all kinds of other stuff is in there, we may look large, malformed, *inflamed*. And, we may certainly feel it. We need deliverance from captivity.

No, I'm not saying that every slim person is Godly, and the opposite applies to others. But what I am saying is that we fast for a reason. That fasting is resistance against the evil inhabitants that want to live in and corrupt our guts. Fasting effects a Godly cleanse and a spiritual purge. Even the world has their own version of this, but if a fast is not dedicated to God, it can be absconded by the dark side and used against you as worship to the kingdom of Satan.

Sex in the Dream?

For of this sort are they which creep into houses,
and lead captive silly women laden with sins, led
away with divers lusts, (2 Timothy 3:6)

You are in captivity. The prison guards are
having their way with you, even pimping you out to
others and other entities. You may be fully aware and
horrified about this, or you may not know a thing about
it. They can wipe your memory of your dreams.
Especially for this reason we need the Holy Spirit who
will bring all things back to our remembrance. Why
would we want to know if we are having sex in the
dream?

So we can pray about it and get rid of any night
husbands, night wives, spirit spouses. Being led into
sins, especially sexual sin does not have to be in this
one dimension of the Earth realm. Pray to the Lord and
ask Him to show you if you have a spirit spouse. Then
dare to ask, *How many?* Also, while you're at it, ask
Him if you have any spirit children, and to show them
to you.

There is an evil summons where your spirit
man, especially if it is weak, can be called to the

craziest places at night while you are asleep. You know that little jump that happens sometimes when you are just falling asleep – that is your spirit man returning from wherever it has been. You shouldn't be wandering around anywhere in your sleep, except to be present with the Lord, but the evils summons may call a person to a graveyard, a satanic circle, a coven, an evil council meeting. You don't know, all of that could be wiped from your memory by the time you wake up.

Sleep paralysis is often for the purpose of demons having sex in the dream, we should call it rape, no one in their right mind would want to have sex with a demon. If you are being sexually assaulted, whether you are a man or a woman, you are captive; you are a spiritual prisoner.

The way to avoid this is to build yourself up spiritually. Also there are good prayers to get out of captivity in this book, and especially toward the back of this book. Foremost, avoid sexual sin in the natural. Being married and drinking waters out of your own cistern--, being faithful to the spouse of your youth will protect you from so much captivity, especially captivity that spawns from sexual sins and illicit relations.

It is better to marry than to burn.

Where Is Your *Real* Spouse?

For, lo, our fathers have fallen by the sword, and our
sons and our daughters and our
wives *are* in **captivity** for this. (2 Chronicles 29:9)

Where is your **real** spouse? Could they be in
captivity? Are you praying for them? Have you
prayed for them? Why aren't you married?

**Could be you are in captivity and the
Captor won't let you marry.**

Where have all the men gone? Where have all
the good men gone? Women, don't be deceived, men
are asking the same question, Where are all the good
women?

Therefore my people are gone
into **captivity**, because *they have* no knowledge: and
their honourable men *are* famished, and their
multitude dried up with thirst. (Isaiah 5:13)

They say that you marry the person that you
want to work out your "stuff" with... Well, your
person has stuff to. Do you intend to be married and
not pray for your spouse. Instead of getting annoyed
with all the stuff that's wrong with your spouse, aren't
you praying for them?

Specifically, are you praying for their deliverance? Are you praying them out of captivity?

Naked, and ye clothed me: I was sick, and ye visited me: I was in prison, and ye came unto me. (Matthew 25:36)

When I was young, I remember the pastor often telling the congregation to visit the sick and shut-in. Should we not also visit and pray for, and even pray for the deliverance of those in spiritual prison, as well as those who are naturally shut in.

What's wrong with most of us is due to spiritual captivity. Things we are programmed, told to do or made to do most often unbeknownst to us. That person may say, "We just act like this, we don't know why.

Uh… it's Captivity.

Instead of pitching fits and moaning about your horrible spouse and then filing for divorce, learn something: Your spouse is most likely in captivity and that is why they do the things they do, or don't do the things they should. You may also be in captivity. If both of you are in Captivity and trying to have a successful marriage – LORD HAVE MERCY. This will be nothing but torment until you both get delivered.

Of course, the enemy wants to break up marriages, so don't fall into the same old trap; get out of captivity. Both of you, get delivered. Don't say that your spouse is the problem, only. Do not be judgmental.

Where Are Your Children?

Thou shalt beget sons and daughters, but thou shalt not enjoy them; for they shall go into **captivity**.
(Deuteronomy 28:41)

WHAT!

No one wants or expects their child to go into captivity. Else, why would you have them? Your goal is not to make them miserable. Most often, we want a better life for our children than we have for ourselves.

If your children are in captivity, that may be because of you. Was Cain not in captivity? Did he not do devilish things, including murder? Was he under control of the Serpent whom Adam and Eve worshipped, or had worshipped at least once that we know of? Wasn't Adam and Eve's punishment the loss of something? Paradise. Authority. Control. Freedom. Position. Glory & Honor? And now their work was going to be hard toil? Tribute. Working for nothing, working to eat—like a hand to mouth curse?

I still do not see where Adam nor Eve attempted to apologize or repent for their behavior, so outside the Garden Eden is spiritual prison? The whole thing?

On a vacation cruise we stopped at a certain port, but we were told, Don't go outside these gates. Outside the gates was deemed unsafe and was a no-go area. People were standing beyond the open slatted iron fences waving their goods and wares that they wanted to also sell to the travelers, but we were told to only buy from the two or three little shops inside the gates. Should we suppose that inside is paradise, and outside is chaos? That's like two different dimensions, two different experiences side by side. Separated only by a gate, and a guard.

So, should mankind's goal be to get back into the Garden, where everything is ordered and beautiful and efficiently works? You know, the Garden that is now guarded by an angel with a sword that turns every which way.

Abel was sacrificed and at the hands of his own brother. Sin was at the gate all the while, crouched, waiting. Don't go outside these gates, these parameters, these laws. The devil had captured Cain's mind; that is where he got the thought to kill his brother, Abel. The devil may have captured other body parts as well, such as his leg. This could be why Abel's offering was accepted by God, and Cain's was not successful.

So, when you see your children suffer it is not so you can feel guilty and beat yourself up, it is so you can learn and repent. It is so you can repent before you even have children. Repent before you even get married. Both of you, get yourselves out of captivity, else your child could be born and then raised in captivity.

Perhaps you were such a child. You may not need to ask the Lord, were you born into poverty, lack, or insufficiency? Was there sickness in your household? Generational diseases? Were you born and raised in anything that even resembles the Curse of the Law? Then you were born in Captivity. That is generational. That is automatic. That is foundational, but you can get out through Christ Jesus and deliverance, amen.

Her adversaries are the chief, her enemies prosper; for the LORD hath afflicted her for the multitude of her transgressions: her children are gone into **captivity** before the enemy. (Lamentations 1:5)

The above verse speaks of a nation, whose children – her people have gone into captivity. But we can personalize this, as all who are in captivity are not in collective captivity, of a nation or even of a family or community; some are individuals.

The LORD is righteous; for I have rebelled against his commandment: hear, I pray you, all people, and behold my sorrow: my virgins and my young men are gone into **captivity**. (Lamentations 1:18)

Where Is Your *Stuff*?

If your stuff is missing, gone, stolen, can't find it, can't seem to get your hands on it, it probably has been taken by the Captor. That is one of the reasons that people are captured in the first place. The enemy wants to get their *stuff*. Even if the enemy is after that man's soul and destiny, if he is captured, there is tribute to pay—so stuff will be taken from that captive. You may not (yet) exhibit even one sign in your body of having been captured, but your wealth, finances and *stuff* is lacking, insufficient, or totally missing: you've been captured.

And they required tribute.

This is why marauding armies attack and capture people, towns, cities, and nations, to raid them, plunder them, take their **stuff**.

Where is your *stuff*?

Have you been captured?

Are you working like an elephant and eating like an ant?

Captured.

Everything you set your hands to should prosper. Is it? If not you know the answer.

You've been captured.

There is so much poverty, so many people in poverty in the world --- I venture to say, they have ALL been captured. The whole world lies in darkness. Now, we don't want to correlate being saved with having money and finances because there are a whole lot of people who are rich as all get out who didn't get what they got from God. Many of them know that they didn't get it from God and will give God no props and no glory.

Many of them know exactly where they got their wealth—the devil. For this reason we cannot assume that people who have money and wealth are godly people because too often they are not.

How can you build a house and not live in it? If you are in prison and the house is not in prison. Captured. So whatever you are asking God for, make sure you know where you will be to receive that thing you've prayed and asked for. Don't you choose the address where you will be to receive your Amazon packages? How many tags will be left on your door, as undeliverable? Do you KNOW for certain where you will be? This could be why you don't have some of your stuff; your stuff couldn't locate you in Captivity, or couldn't or wouldn't deliver in Captivity, knowing that you'd never get it. It would be snatched from you.

How can you earn money and not get to see it or touch it or use it? If you are in prison—on a chain gang, the guards and warden are making you work but taking everything or most of everything you make. Captured.

Rich people who you may believe are not giving you a chance are not necessarily your problem. You may think they are your task masters; they may not be that at all. They may be in captivity themselves, after all, they are guarding you. They are stealing from you. God doesn't send people to steal, that's not His shtick. The devil steals.

The wealthy man may be an agent of Satan, he may not be. He could be blessed and highly favored of the Lord. You cannot suppose that because he has money that he is blessed and favored of God. He may be an evil agent, fully aware of such or unawares. The devil may be rewarding him. You will know him by his fruit. Fruit of the Spirit – does he have any? Does he exhibit any? Observe that person in private, observe him when he doesn't think anyone is looking, if at all possible. You can't judge a person by what he does in public; it could all be a show.

All of us are taught to put on our best behavior in public—we are taught to act, really. Where we should be taught to be, we are taught to behave, or act like we have home training and good sense, and manners. You know, all the stuff our parents said to us when they took us places, so we didn't embarrass them or get kicked out of school.

The wealth of the wicked is laid up for the just. You aren't wicked, are you? Then why are you suffering the punishment of the wicked? And, even in this life? Isn't this life supposed to be abundant and the forerunner of life eternal? You don't want eternity to be like this if you are in captivity, do you? Perhaps all of this life is a clue as to where you will spend eternity and how you will spend it if you don't get it together. People think they must simply trudge along and endure and then Glory will be magic. Folks believe they will get wings of a bird to fly away--- well first we need to get ourselves out of captivity. No caged bird flies away. A caged bird is dinner.

The more ungodly your behavior, the more likely you are captive; the more captive you probably are. Whether you want to do right but can't, or you don't even want to do right – captive. The more wrong you want to do the more captive you are.

Yet within the prison of your captivity, if you have risen among the ranks, the more indoctrinated, the more incarcerated, the more captive you are.

Joseph – God was with him, and he rose everywhere he went, but Joseph never *became* an Egyptian. In captivity. Joseph did get out of the prison. The goal in prison is to get you to take on the nature of your captor. Joseph never did. You don't need to stay in captivity – the Lord will deliver.

The whole world lies in darkness. Darkness, for the most part, is accompanied by poverty.

Financial bondages, embargoes. Stuck. Captive. Rope over rope, over rope. Captivity is so you will be ripped off and stolen from, that could be based on what you have or what you are going to have, even what your children and their children will earn in their lives. Captivity leads to poverty, but there is a poverty that leads to captivity as well. When chronically impoverished get desperate they make seek desperate measures. This is the making of a criminal. A criminal is a natural way of saying sinner, which is the spiritual term. Now, here comes another rope, or chain, or padlock, or whatever device is being used to hold you. *Hold still; stay here so I can do more stuff to you,* the devil is probably saying to the captive.

Grow Stronger

Then answered they and said before the king, That
Daniel, which *is* of the children of the captivity of
Judah, regardeth not thee, O king, nor the decree
that thou hast signed, but maketh his petition three
times a day.(Daniel 6:13)

Yes, this was a deep dive into captivity, and I
won't leave you without leading you into how to get
out of captivity, as I have attempted to do throughout
this volume. Daniel and his friends were captive in
Babylon by Nebuchadnezzar. Studying them is a
picture of what spiritual captivity must be like. The
goal is to break the prisoner down, wear him out, kill
him if possible. Yet Daniel and his friends grew
stronger and they were ten times better than those who
followed the prison mandates.

In captivity the captor does not want you to
pray; SO PRAY. A prayer watch is three hours. Jesus
asked His Disciples to intercede for him for one hour,
but that is a bare minimum. Do a full watch of prayers,
if not all at once, pray for an hour three times a day;
that's what Daniel did. Praying at dawn, noon, and
6pm or midnight is a good format and start. When you
up your prayer life, besides inflammation, saints of

God, afflictions will drop off. Even long-time afflictions, which is indication in the natural that you are being spiritually delivered. Captivity against you will be weakened, and eventually you will be set free. How did Daniel become a prime minister in Babylon? He was set free. Like Joseph--, set free.

In captivity the captor does not want you to read your Bible; SO READ YOUR BIBLE, especially out loud. Demons hate this. Yes, the Word will set you free, but the demons can hardly wait to see you go. Not only that, when a deliverance minister comes to you, the more Word in you, the easier it is for you to be delivered.

In captivity the captor does not want you to praise or worship God; SO PRAISE and WORSHIP GOD. Paul and Silas got out of jail by praising God.

We've talked about what you eat already in the chapter, *You're Being Fed?* Spiritual prison food is not something you want to ingest, and what has been swallowed needs to be vomited out.

In captivity, the captor does not want you to tithe or give offerings. Argue with me all you want, but you should tithe and give offerings. This can get a little tricky because you have to be SURE that you're SURE, by the Spirit of God that you are giving to a Godly place.

Now, if you are really in captivity, doing any one or all of these things will cause opposition in your natural life. You have to press through that opposition if you ever want to get out of captivity. Recall, that captivity can last a long time, a lifetime; it is a war. Even so you do not want to play with this. Your life, your whole life and the lives of your children and your entire bloodline may depend on you getting yourself out of captivity.

Grow stronger by reading your Bible **out loud**. Oh the devil hates this. If you cannot physically sit yourself down and read, go online and let someone read the Bible to you. After you've read it all the way through, read it again.

You may choose a different translation when you next read through the Bible in order to gain more insight in, and revelation from what you are reading.

Choose your Bible well. Choose your translation well. Bibles made in countries that do not even believe in God are very unwise choices; they have an ungodly anointing on them. Former witches and warlocks advise not to use Bibles with red covers. The KJV is the best version, but read what you can understand.

Especially read Psalm 2, Psalm 24, Psalm 29, Psalm 35, Psalm 57 and Psalm 99 out loud. Actually this combo, in this order is very powerful. Praying the Word of God is always very powerful.

Interface with the Holy Spirit of God. If you do not yet have the Holy Spirit pray for Him to infill you. If you have the Holy Spirit, then ask for a fresh infilling, or fresh anointing every day.

If my people, which are called by my name, shall humble themselves, and pray, and seek my face, and turn from their wicked ways; then will I hear from heaven, and will forgive their sin, and will heal their land. (2 Chronicles 7:14)

A healed land is a delivered land. Also, you are made of the clay of the Earth; you are the land.

Ask God for the Nations

Ask of me, and I will give thee the nations for thine
inheritance, and the uttermost parts of the earth for
thy possession. (Psalm 2:8)

If you ever come to yourself, if you ever realize
that you are captive, it you realize your authority in
Christ and that you can get out of there you will have
a righteous indignation. You will have a new boldness.
You will pray differently, you will speak differently,
you will begin to rise up in your authority and do
warfare.

You will ask God for the **nations**.

Why do the heathen rage, and the people imagine a
vain thing? The kings of the earth set themselves,
and the rulers take counsel together, against
the Lord, and against his anointed, saying,

Let us break their bands asunder, and cast away
their cords from us. He that sitteth in the heavens
shall laugh: the Lord shall have them in derision.
(Psalm 2:1-4)

The devil is the prince of this world and he has
rulers, and principalities and powers under him. The
nations are countries in the natural, but in the spirit
world the nations are thrones and spiritual wickedness

in high places. Nations are demons, devils, and idol gods. Nations are what captures people and holds them captive. While captive, if they can extract things of value from you, they will. They seek things of monetary value, things of spiritual value such as your gifts, skills, abilities, and virtues. They seek future gifts, such as your blessings from God. They seek your destiny, your legacy, even your children and grandchildren, as well as your marital destiny. The nations, so many to be counted can be your captors.

But, as Jesus took captivity captive, then so you must also do the same if they are not following the prescription Jesus established on Calvary, by defeating Death in Hell and resurrecting. The nations must be defeated spiritually.

Ask the Lord, according to Psalm 2 to give you the nations. He says he will do it. You need the authority back—that you used to have over those who have taken authority over you. If you are not exercising your spiritual authority over the enations when you were free, that is most likely how you got captured. Don't wait until you get old and everything is hurting, and physical symptoms are over the top – all that is captivity and because of captivity. We should all be aging gracefully. Sickness, illness, death – they are all under the curse of the law and we are all redeemed from that. Walk in it.

57. Lord, I repent of my sins, the sins of my parents and my ancestors all the way back to Adam and Eve, Lord forgive my bloodline and take away the iniquity, in the Name of Jesus.

58. Lord, set me free from whatever has me bound, in the Name of Jesus.

59. Lord set me free from wherever I am being held captive, in the Name of Jesus.

60. Lord, buy me back from wherever they have sold me, in the Name of Jesus.

61. Lord, I cease and desist from all worldly endeavors such as seeking wealth, fame, power or social influence, in the Name of Jesus.

62. Lord, I cease all obsessions with sports, music, celebrities, and entertainment, in the Name of Jesus.

63. I resist all things that have captured my mind or imagination, in the Name of Jesus.

64. Lord, deliver me from the powers of familial, ancestral, cultural, and generational traditions, in the Name of Jesus.

65. Lord, deliver me from competition, peer pressure and every other work of the flesh, in the Name of Jesus.

66. Every strongman jailer be bound by mighty warrior angels of God and let me go, in the Name of Jesus.

67. Every barrier, obstacle, cage, bars, blocking me, holding me captive, limiting me, keeping me from progressing, burn with Holy Ghost Fire and be removed, and let me go, in the Name of Jesus.

68. Every marine kingdom prison holding me, I break every evil covenant made with you that has allowed me to be captured, and I break free by the power in the Blood of Jesus.

69. Captivity because of flesh addictions of any kind, I break your bondage, I break your yokes holding me, I break free, by the power in the Blood of Jesus, in the Name of Jesus.

70. Alcohol, drugs, sex, works of the flesh, any sin, Lord deliver me, by Your power, by Your Spirit, bring me out of this prison, bring me out of every prison, in the Name of Jesus.

71. Lord, search the land of the living and the dead, find me, and bring me out of every

captivity. I vow to serve You and only You from this day forth, in the Name of Jesus.

72. Unforgiveness holding me captive, where I've tried to hold someone else captive, LORD, I forgive them; Lord, forgive me and let me go free from this hell, in the Name of Jesus.

73. Bitterness, I bind you, you shall no longer keep me captive, in the Name of Jesus.

74. Resentment, I bind you, you shall no longer keep me captive, in the Name of Jesus.

75. Jealousy, I bind you, you shall no longer keep me captive, in the Name of Jesus.

76. Pride, I bind you, you shall no longer keep me captive, in the Name of Jesus.

77. Greed, I bind you, you shall no longer hold me captive, in the Name of Jesus.

78. Lust, I bind you and break your hold over me; you shall no longer hold me as your prisoner, in the Name of Jesus.

79. Anger, I bind and paralyze your effects over me, you shall no longer have control over me, my emotions, my life. I go free, in the Name of Jesus.

80. Competition , extreme competition, you are bound and paralyzed to work against my mind. I am delivered, in the Name of Jesus.

81. Grief, extreme grief, pining away, I thank God for the times that I had who I had in my life and what I had in my life, if it is now gone, I release it fully, and I am disconnected from it in a Godly way and I go free to live and declare the goodness of the Lord, in the Land of the Living, in the Name of Jesus.

82. Every disease, disorder, illness, sickness, syndrome and symptom because of Captivity, fall away from me now; I am healed by the Blood of Jesus. I am made whole, in Christ Jesus; Amen.

83. Error, be bound, be paralyzed, shut your mouth. Don't say another thing to me. I am in Christ; I have the Mind of Christ and the Spirit of God. I am led into all Truth, and I will no longer believe a lie---, not one lie. The Truth has and will always set me free: I go free, in the Name of Jesus.

84. Every loss or missed opportunity I have suffered because of Captivity, Lord. restore me, by Your Mercy, by Your Grace, and by Your strength, in the Name of Jesus.

85. By the authority of Christ Jesus, I bind and remove the guards and with the keys of every kind of Captivity, I open every door, gate, chain, fetter, iron, padlock, or anything that has me bound, and I break out of Captivity, in the Name of Jesus.

86. If my spirit man has been entombed, I remove the Stone, even every stone of offense, int eh Name of Jesus.

87. If my spirit man has been buried, I jump out of that grave that was prepared for me, in the Name of Jesus.

88. If my spirit man was submerged under water, I jump out of every water, any water that tried to hold me, and I go free, in the Name of Jesus.

89. Mighty Angels of the Lord God, take my soul out of captivity, take my soul of Hell (X7).

90. Search the land of the living and the dead for all my humanity, and return it to me, in the Name of Jesus.

91. Remove me from any burial or grave, in the Name of Jesus.

His Mercy

> That then the LORD thy God will
> turn thy **captivity,** and have compassion upon thee,
> and will return and gather thee from all the
> nations, whither the LORD thy God hath
> scattered thee. (Deuteronomy 30:3)

Even if you do everything prescribed in the last chapter to break out of captivity, it will still take the Love, Mercy and Grace of God to get you out of there. **Not by power, nor by might, but by my Spirit** says the Lord. The Lord's Spirit is the Spirit of Mercy. The Lord's Spirit is the Spirit of Love; God is Love. The Lord's Spirit is the Spirit of Grace; Jesus grew more in stature and Grace daily. Note that of all the things mentioned the greatest of these is Love. Also notice that the devil has absolutely NONE of those things; No Mercy. No Grace. No Love. In the balance of things, if the devil has none, then God has all. So there you go. All power also belongs to God, but by His Spirit, the Holy Spirit of God are we delivered.

> Yet *if* they bethink themselves in the land whither
> they are carried captive, and turn and pray unto
> thee in the land of their **captivity,** saying, We have

sinned, we have done amiss, and have dealt wickedly;

If they return to thee with all their heart and with all their soul in the land of their **captivity**, whither they have carried them captives, and pray toward their land, which thou gavest unto their fathers, and *toward* the city which thou hast chosen, and toward the house which I have built for thy name: (2 Chronicles 6:38-37)

92. Lord, have Mercy on me, a sinner. I am caught up, I am captured. Lord, I need deliverance. With all my heart and soul, with everything that is in me, I repent; I am sorry please forgive me, rescue me from this captivity so that I may again serve You with my whole heart, in the Name of Jesus.

Oh that the salvation of Israel *were come* out of Zion! when the LORD bringeth back the **captivity** of his people, Jacob shall rejoice, *and* Israel shall be glad. (Psalm 14:7)

93. Lord, I pray to You, out of Zion, bring me back from captivity and I will rejoice and forever praise You. Lord, make my heart glad again, I turn from my wicked ways, in the Name of Jesus.

Oh that the salvation of Israel *were come* out of Zion! When God bringeth back the **captivity** of his people, Jacob shall rejoice, *and* Israel shall be glad. (Psalm 53:6)

LORD, thou hast been favourable unto thy
land: thou hast brought back the **captivity** of Jacob.
(Psalm 85:1B)

94. Lord, Your favor is life. Be favorable to me, O
    Lord, bring me back from hell and its
    captivity, in the Name of Jesus.

When the LORD turned again the **captivity** of
Zion, we were like them that dream.

Turn again our **captivity**, O LORD, as the streams in
the south. (Psalm 126:1,4)

95. Lord, do not leave my soul in hell, turn now
    my captivity, for it is more than I can bear, in
    the Name of Jesus.

For, lo, the days come, saith the LORD, that I will
bring again the **captivity** of my people Israel and
Judah, saith the LORD: and I will cause them to
return to the land that I gave to their fathers, and
they shall possess it. (Jeremiah 30:3)

96. Lord, declare a new season in my life, one of
    liberation, freedom, and peace. Return my
    captivity that I may come up and worship You
    with my whole heart, in the Beauty of Your
    Holiness, in the Name of Jesus.

Therefore fear thou not, O my
servant Jacob, saith the LORD; neither be
dismayed, O Israel: for, lo, I will save thee from
afar, and thy seed from the land of
their **captivity**; and Jacob shall return, and shall be
in rest, and be quiet, and none shall
make *him* afraid. (Jeremiah 30:10)

97. Save O Lord. Save me. I am in desolation in a far away land that I know not of. Let me return to be at rest and quiet that no one again shall ever make me afraid. You are the Lord. In the Name of Jesus, I pray.

Thus saith the LORD of hosts, the God of Israel; As yet they shall use this speech in the land of Judah and in the cities thereof, when I shall bring again their **captivity**; The LORD bless thee, O habitation of justice, *and* mountain of holiness. (Jeremiah 31:23)

98. Lord, bless me and bless my habitation with Peace. Bless me Lord, release me from this captivity that I may serve You in Your holiness.

Men shall buy fields for money, and subscribe evidences, and seal *them*, and take witnesses in the land of Benjamin, and in the places about Jerusalem, and in the cities of Judah, and in the cities of the mountains, and in the cities of the valley, and in the cities of the south: for I will cause their **captivity** to return, saith the LORD. (Jeremiah 32:44)

99. Return my captivity Lord, that I may prosper in the land that you have given me and my generations, in the Name of Jesus.

And I will cause the **captivity** of Judah and the **captivity** of Israel to return, and will build them, as at the first. (Jeremiah 33:7)

100.   Return Lord, my captivity and build me that Your Name may be glorified in the land of the living. In the Name of Jesus, Amen.

The voice of joy, and the voice of gladness, the voice of the bridegroom, and the voice of the bride, the voice of them that shall say, Praise the LORD of hosts: for the LORD *is* good; for his mercy *endureth* for ever: *and* of them that shall bring the sacrifice of praise into the house of the LORD. For I will cause to return the **captivity** of the land, as at the first, saith the LORD.
(Jeremiah 33:11)

101.   Praise the Lord of Hosts, for the Lord is good and His Mercy endures forever. Lord, I praise you even in the midnight, even in chains I will praise You. O Lord, bring me out that I may offer sacrifices of praise and thanksgiving. *Loose* these bands of captivity, O Lord, and bring me out, in the Name of Jesus.

Then will I cast away the seed of Jacob, and David my servant, *so* that I will not take *any* of his seed *to be* rulers over the seed of Abraham, Isaac, and Jacob: for I will cause their **captivity** to return, and have mercy on them.
(Jeremiah 33:26)

102.   Have Mercy on me, Thou Son of David; Have Mercy on me, Thou Son of God. Free me from this iniquity and its punishments, in the Name of Jesus.

The punishment of thine iniquity is accomplished, O daughter of Zion; he will no more carry thee away into **captivity**: he will visit thine iniquity, O daughter of Edom; he will discover thy sins. (Lamentations 4:22)

103.　　Lord, declare an end to this captivity. Free me, so that I may be free indeed, in the Name of Jesus.

And the coast shall be for the remnant of the house of Judah; they shall feed thereupon: in the houses of Ashkelon shall they lie down in the evening: for the LORD their God shall visit them, and turn away their **captivity**. (Zephaniah 2:7)

104.　　Jehovah Rohee; You are the God who sees me. Lord, look on me and deliver me from those who are too strong for me, by Your Mighty Right Hand, in the Name of Jesus.

At that time will I bring you *again*, even in the time that I gather you: for I will make you a name and a praise among all people of the earth, when I turn back your **captivity** before your eyes, saith the LORD. (Zephaniah 3:20)

105.　　Lord, I have been scattered. I have been scattered abroad and scattered about. Lord, turn back my captivity and gather me as a hen would gather her chicks. Locate me and put me back together; remember me, O Lord, in the Name of Jesus.

Therefore thus saith the Lord GOD; Now will I bring again the captivity of Jacob, and have mercy upon

the whole house of Israel, and will be jealous for my
holy name; (Ezekiel 39:25)

106.   Lord, have Mercy on me and my whole
house. I am in Jacob and You are the One who
forgives Jacob. Lord, bring me out of captivity
and I also will jealously guard Your laws and
precepts, and I will walk upright and not turn
from Your ways, in the Name of Jesus.

Then shall they know that I *am* the LORD their
God, which caused them to be led
into captivity among the heathen: but I have
gathered them unto their own land, and have
left none of them any more there. (Ezekiel 39:28)

107.   You are the Lord; gather me from
these heathens that I may again walk free and
upright, and unencumbered by evil
oppressors, in the Name of Jesus.

Also, O Judah, he hath set an harvest for thee, when
I returned the captivity of my people. (Hosea 6:11)

108.   Lord of the Harvest, Lord of great
abundance, release and restore me double for
all this trouble. I will guard my ways to honor
You from now on, in the Name of Jesus.

For, behold, in those days, and in that time, when I
shall bring again the captivity of Judah and
Jerusalem, (Joel 3:1)

All my bones shall say, Lord, who is like unto thee,
which deliverest the poor from him that is too
strong for him, yea, the poor and the needy from
him that spoileth him? (Psalm 35)

God Will Repay

He that leadeth into **captivity** shall
go into **captivity**: he that killeth with the
sword must be killed with the sword. Here is the
patience and the faith of the saints.
(Revelations 13:10)

Saints of God, even if you are the cause of your captivity--, no matter who was the cause, if God allowed the captivity, He was using it. Using it to teach you? Possibly. Using it as punishment? Punishment is built into sin, and God cannot lie. Surely it grieved Him to do so, as it would any parent, but God corrects those He loves; He disciplines them. To prune you? Yes. To purify and refine you? Yes.

But know that the captor or captors that took you into captivity will surely also be judged and punished. How is that? God knows evil; God sees evil. God judges evil. If He allows or has allowed evil, it is because He was using it for any or all the reasons in the above paragraph.

As with the devil, however, if allowed a little, he will take more and more and eventually try to take all. God then waits until their iniquity is full to judge them. This is why vengeance belongs to God and should not be undertaken by humans. Revenge plans are in the flesh and will be invaded by and anointed by the devil, taking them over the top with no Mercy whatsoever. God neither responds nor reacts in the flesh; God is Spirit; therefore, retribution is balanced and purposeful when left in the hands of God.

Our God is a God of balance and just weights. He is a God of Mercy and Vengeance. Man cannot boast of that when he is demonically driven by the flesh because in our flesh dwells no good thing.

Therefore all they that devour thee shall be devoured; and all thine adversaries, every one of them, shall go into **captivity**; and they that spoil thee shall be a spoil, and all that prey upon thee will I give for a prey. (Jeremiah 30:16)

But fear not thou, O my servant Jacob, and be not dismayed, O Israel: for, behold, I will save thee from afar off, and thy seed from the land of their **captivity**; and Jacob shall return, and be in rest and at ease, and none shall make *him* afraid. (Jeremiah 46:27)

I will break also the bar of Damascus, and cut off the inhabitant from the plain of Aven, and him that holdeth the sceptre from the house of Eden: and the people of Syria shall go into captivity unto Kir, saith the LORD.

Thus saith the LORD; For three transgressions of Gaza, and for four, I will not turn away *the punishment* thereof; because they carried away

captive the whole captivity, to deliver *them* up to
Edom: (Amos 1:5-6)

I have no pity on him, but to go from Heavenly
Worship leader to jailer – what a fall. Saints of God be
sure that you don't go from worshipper to being jailed
in the spirit. That can happen if you are worshipping
the wrong thing, the wrong things, and the wrong *god*.

Even if you do, and you go through the **_most_**,
know with assurance that those who captured you,
those who tormented or tortured you, those who held
you captive--, the devil and the third of the stars that
fell from Heaven, and their evil human agents will be
repaid. And, they know it.

And the devil that deceived them was cast into the
lake of fire and brimstone, where the beast and the
false prophet are, and shall be tormented day and
night for ever and ever. (Revelations 20:10)

Where will you be when all that goes down?
<u>ALL</u> **of you?** Get out of Captivity--, every part of
you, get out of Captivity now, before it is too late.

Dear Reader

     Thank you and God bless you for acquiring and reading this book. Now that you have a roadmap, **Get Out of Captivity.**

In the Name of Jesus,

Amen.

Dr. Marlene Miles

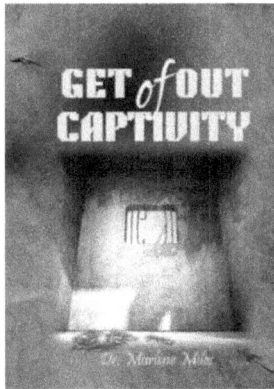

Footnotes:

a. 1 Kings 20:32; Joshua 10:24; Judges 1:7; 2 Sam. 4:12; Judges 8:7; 2 Sam 12:31; 1 Chronicles 20:3).

b. Matthew 5:28,

c. Also see, Lamentations 1:3-5 and Ezekiel 39:23-24.

d. 2 Kings 15:19-20; 1 Chronicles 5:26; 762 B.C. and 738 B.C.

e. 2 Kings 15:29; Isaiah 9:1.

f. 2 Kings 1:3, 5; 721 B. C.

g. 2 Kings 24:13; Jeremiah 24:1; 2 Chronicles 36:10

h. 2 Chronicles 36:22; Ezra 1:2

i. B.C. 598 B.C.

j. Also, . (Matthew 13:42; 13:50; 22:13, 24:51, 25:30; Luke 13:28)

Source: Easton's Bible Dictionary

Other Prayer books by this author.

While most books by this author have prayer points either throughout the book or at the end, there are some books that are only prayers. You just open up the book and pray. They are listed below:

Prayers Against Barrenness: *For Success in Business and Life*

Fruit of the Womb: *Prayers Against Barrenness*

Beauty Curses, *Warfare Prayers Against*
https://a.co/d/5Xlc20M

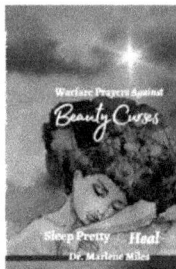

Courts of Marriage: Prayers for Marriage in the Courts of Heaven *(prayerbook)* https://a.co/d/cNAdgAq

Courtroom Warfare @ Midnight *(prayerbook)*
https://a.co/d/5fc7Qdp

Demonic Cobwebs *(prayerbook)* https://a.co/d/fp9Oa2H

Every Evil Bird https://a.co/d/hF1kh1O

Gates of Thanksgiving

Spirits of Death, Hell & the Grave, Pass Over Me and My House

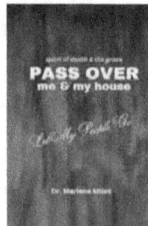

Throne of Grace: Courtroom Prayer

Warfare Prayer Against Poverty
https://a.co/d/bZ611Yu

Other books by this author

AK: The Adventures of the Agape Kid

AMONG SOME THIEVES

Ancestral Powers

Anti-Marriage, The Spirit of

Backstabbers https://a.co/d/gi8iBxf

Barrenness, *Prayers Against*
https://a.co/d/feUltIs

Battlefield of Marriage, *The*

Blindsided: *Has the Old Man Bewitched You?*
https://a.co/d/5O2fLLR

Break Free from Collective Captivity

Casting Down Imaginations

Churchzilla, The Wanna-Be, Supposed-to-be
Bride of Christ

Curses of Blind Men

Demonic Cobwebs (prayerbook)

Demonic Time Bombs

Demons Hate Questions

Devil Loves Trauma, *The*

Devil Weapons: Unforgiveness, Bitterness,…

The Devourers: Thieves of Darkness 2

Do Not Swear by the Moon

Don't Refuse Me, Lord (4 book series)
https://a.co/d/idP34LG

Dream Defilement

The Emptiers: *Thieves of Darkness, 1*
https://a.co/d/5I4n5mc

Evil Touch

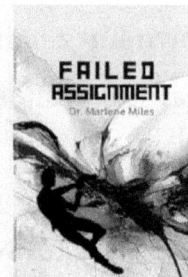

Failed Assignment

Fantasy Spirit Spouse https://a.co/d/hW7oYbX

FAT Demons (The): *Breaking Demonic Curses*

The Fold (5-book series)

- The Fold (Book 1)
- Name Your Seed (Book 2)
- The Poor Attitudes of Money (3)
- Do Not Orphan Your Seed (4)
- For the Sake of the Gospel (5)
- My Sowing Journal

Gang Ups: Touch Not God's Anointed

Give Us This Day

got HEALING? Verses for Life

got LOVE? Verses for Life

got HOPE? Verses for Life

got money? https://a.co/d/g2av41N

How to Dental Assist

How to Dental Assist2: Be Productive, Not Wasteful

I Take It Back

Legacy

Let Me Have A Dollar's Worth
https://a.co/d/h8F8XgE

Let Them Come Up & Worship

Level the Playing Field

Living for the NOW of God

Lose My Location https://a.co/d/crD6mV9

Man Safari, *The*

Marriage Ed. Rules of Engagement & Marriage

Made Perfect in Love

Money Hunters: Beware of Those

Money on the Altar https://a.co/d/4EqJ2Nr

Mulberry Tree https://a.co/d/9nR9rRb

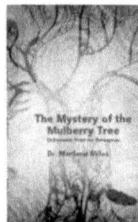

Motherboard (The) - *Soul Prosperity Series*

Name Your Seed

Occupy: *Until I Return*

Plantation Souls

Players Gonna Play

Power Money: Nine Times the Tithe

https://a.co/d/gRt41gy

The Power of Wealth *(forthcoming)*

Powers Above

The Robe, Part 1, The Lessons of Joseph

The Robe, Part II, The Lessons of Joseph

Seasons of Grief

Seasons of Waiting

Seasons of War

Second Marriage, Third~~, *Any Marriage*

https://a.co/d/6m6GN4N

Sift You Like Wheat

Six Men Short: What Has Happened to all the Men?

Soul Prosperity, soul prosperity series 3

https://a.co/d/5p8YvCN

Souls Captivity soul prosperity series 2

The Spirit of Anti-Marriage

The Spirit of Poverty

StarStruck

SUNBLOCK

The Swallowers: *Thieves of Darkness*, 3

Take It Back

This Is NOT That: How to Keep Demons from Coming at You

Time Is of the Essence

Too Many Wives: *Why You Have Lady Problems*

Tormenting Spirits   https://a.co/d/dAogEJf

Toxic Souls

Triangular Power *(series)*

- Powers Above
- SUNBLOCK
- Do Not Swear by the Moon
- STARSTRUCK

Uncontested Doom

Unguarded Hours, *The*

Unseen Life, *The* (forthcoming)

Upgrade: How to Get Out of Survival Mode

- Toxic Souls (Book 2 of series)
- Legacy (Book 3 of series)

WTH? Get Me Out of This HELL
https://a.co/d/9sLmCoE

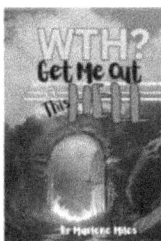

The Wasters: *Thieves of Darkness*, Bk 2
https://a.co/d/bUvI9Jo

What Have You to Declare? What Do You Have With You from Where You've Been?

When I Was A Child, *I Prayed As a Child*

When the Devourer is Rebuked

https://a.co/d/1HVv8oq

The Wilderness Romance *(series)* This series is about conducting a Godly relationship and marriage with someone who is a Wilderness person. It is about how to recognize it and navigate through it. These books are about how not to get caught up in such.

- *The Social Wilderness*
- *The Sexual Wilderness*
- *The Spiritual Wilderness*

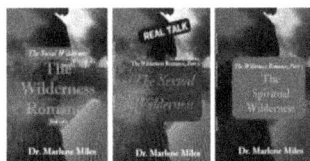

Other Series

The Fold (a series on Godly finances)
https://a.co/d/4hz3unj

Soul Prosperity Series https://a.co/d/bz2M42q

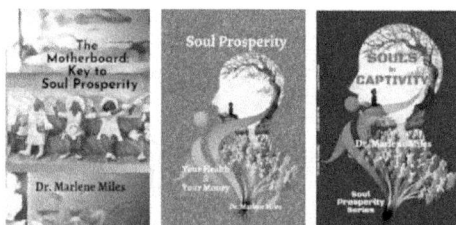

Spirit Spouse books

https://a.co/d/9VehDSo

https://a.co/d/97sKOwm

Thieves of Darkness series

Triangular Powers https://a.co/d/aUCjAWC

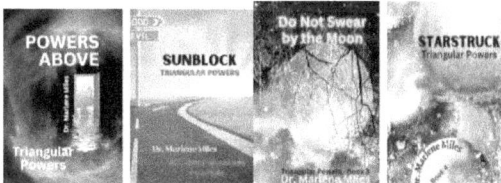

Upgrade (series) *How to Get Out of Survival Mode*
https://a.co/d/aTERhXO

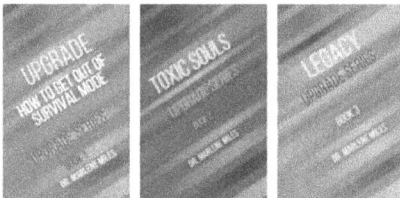

www.ingramcontent.com/pod-product-compliance
Lightning Source LLC
LaVergne TN
LVHW052028080426
835513LV00018B/2231